"My dear friend Jane Hamon has deliver-- ~ powerful must-read! This book ~~~" and move you into action. Jan<  aven that will enable you to t< stolen in every area of your lif

Nancy Alcoi , ...cy Multiplied

"*Confronting the Thief* is a beacon of hope, offering deep insights into reclaiming what's ours from the enemy. Her mastery in unveiling scriptural mysteries empowers us to embrace our divine heritage fully. A truly transformative read, it's essential for anyone seeking to walk in God's fullness. This book is an essential read for anyone eager to confront and overpower the enemy."

Tomi Arayomi, apostle; founder, RIG Nation

"Jane Hamon sagaciously helps us navigate into a place of divine recovery. God desires for us all to experience abundance in every area of life. However, there is an enemy arrayed against our peace and prosperity. This book is a dispensary of prophetic wisdom that will help you overcome the purloining ways of the enemy and supernaturally regain what has been stolen from you."

Demontae A. Edmonds, author, *The Supernatural Dimension of Dreams* and *Discerning of Spirits*

"On many occasions in my journey, a book, a song, a story, a truth, or a person entered my life just when I was ready for the message accompanying it. I often experience this when listening to my friend Jane Hamon's ministry. She utters a simple truth underscored by Holy Spirit insight, and my response is, 'Aha!' *Confronting the Thief* is such a timely and needed now word."

Bishop Joseph L. Garlington, founding pastor,
Covenant Church of Pittsburgh; presiding bishop,
Reconciliation Ministries International

"*Confronting the Thief* is a timely, strategic, prophetic message—a now word! The army is rising to confront and conquer the schemes of Satan. Divine recovery is your Kingdom of heaven inheritance. Be empowered to decree victoriously to take back all the enemy and his army of darkness have stolen."

Rebecca Greenwood, cofounder, Christian Harvest
International and Strategic Prayer Apostolic Network

"If ever there was a book for this hour, it is this one! *Confronting the Thief* is a revelatory work that will release answers to many of your life's challenges. Jane Hamon has hit the nail on the proverbial head in uncovering strongholds that hold back our individual prosperity, health, and well-being. I have never read anything like it! Her research to back the wisdom on demonic strongholds that are stealing from our well-being and that of our family, communities, and nation is impressive. She presents real historical studies, not sketchy assertions. Prepare to be set free from long-standing problems and pain! I know you will be thrilled with the results!"

Cindy Jacobs, Generals International

"Jesus clearly taught, 'The thief comes . . . to steal and kill and destroy' (John 10:10 NIV). Jane Hamon not only brilliantly teaches how the enemy comes but will help you accurately discern him, overcome him, and make him sorry he ever tried! I love Jane Hamon and I love this book! It is timely. It is needed. It is for you!"

Patricia King, minister, author, media producer, and host; PatriciaKing.com

"What a faith-building, strategy-equipping book! Apostle Jane Hamon has masterfully taught us how to identify and confront the thief and recover everything that has been stolen, lost, or hidden. From our purpose to our prosperity to our passion and more, she develops through Scriptures, decrees, and true-life examples what it takes to develop a resolve to deny and dismantle the lie that 'this is just life.'"

Kim Owens, pastor and revivalist; author, *Doorkeepers of Revival* and *Just to Make Religion Mad*

"My friend Jane Hamon has written a revelatory, relatable, transformative, insightful, and practical book filled with a depth and anointing that only comes through years of prayer, study, and experience. It is excellent. Every chapter, every word is valuable. It is a book I will refer to often, a true guidebook to taking back what is rightfully ours. I highly, highly recommend it."

Tim Sheets, apostle; author, *Angel Armies*, *Planting the Heavens*, *Come Home*, and more; pastor, Oasis Church

CONFRONTING
THE
THIEF

TAKE BACK WHAT THE ENEMY STOLE AND
DECLARE DIVINE RECOVERY
OVER YOUR HEART, FAMILY, AND LIFE

JANE HAMON

Chosen
a division of Baker Publishing Group
Minneapolis, Minnesota

Published by Chosen Books
Minneapolis, Minnesota
ChosenBooks.com

Chosen Books is a division of
Baker Publishing Group, Grand Rapids, Michigan

Printed in the United States of America

Library of Congress Cataloging-in-Publication Data
Names: Hamon, Jane, author.
Title: Confronting the thief : take back what the enemy stole and declare divine recovery over your heart, family, and life / Jane Hamon.
Description: Minneapolis, Minnesota : Chosen Books, a division of Baker Publishing Group, [2024] | Includes bibliographical references.
Identifiers: LCCN 2023048317 | ISBN 9780800772451 (paper) | ISBN 9780800772543 (casebound) | ISBN 9781493445653 (ebook)
Subjects: LCSH: Theft—Biblical teaching. | Restitution—Biblical teaching.
Classification: LCC BS680.S76 H36 2024 | DDC 241/.62—dc23/eng/20240129
LC record available at https://lccn.loc.gov/2023048317

Cover design by Rob Williams
Cover image from Shutterstock

Baker Publishing Group publications use paper produced from sustainable forestry practices and postconsumer waste whenever possible.

24 25 26 27 28 29 30   7 6 5 4 3 2 1

CONTENTS

Foreword

have not read a book that I enjoyed as much as *Confronting the Thief*! We are living in a season and time to reclaim and recover what has been lost. Jane Hamon has captured the heart of God for His people in this work.

My whole life is built around the principles of restoration and recovery. Even though I was saved at an early age, I had a difficult and often traumatic and abusive childhood. My family had suffered great loss and anguish. Much of my family fell apart during my teen years as a result of the enemy's inroads into my father's life. He then died under tragic circumstances when I was sixteen. By the time I turned eighteen, working, going to college, and having a fairly ardent nightlife began to take a toll on my body.

Eventually, I wound up in the hospital, suffering from exhaustion and double pneumonia. When I was in the hospital, the Lord clearly spoke to me in an audible voice and said, *"I will restore all that you have lost."* With those words, He penetrated every part of my being. Though I had suspected it before, I now knew that God had a plan not only to go back and heal the wounds of my past but also to restore my future.

I had never seen the concept of restoration in the Bible, but as I began to read more deeply following that encounter, I learned that God's voice has the power to restore (see Joel 2:25). My whole life changed from that moment, and since that time, God has healed, delivered, and restored me in miraculous ways. God's voice has great power to bring us out of the ruins of our past and set us on the course He has ordained for our lives, as I learned on that day many years ago. My life message and ministry worldwide are built on the platform of recovery, restoration, restitution, and redemption.

To recover means "to recuperate or regain what has been lost or taken or to regain your health and get well." In seasons of lost authority, we are called to return to a state of control or authority. As you read Jane's book, let me share seven key issues for you to decree as you take your assigned stand. You may have lost in one season, but now decree this is the time:

1. To save yourself from falling, slipping, or being betrayed
2. To regain or reclaim land, substances from waste
3. To retrieve a person from a bad state
4. To get back by judgment
5. To return to a balance from weakness
6. To cover again
7. To reclaim or demand or decree that restoration of a thing will begin

As we decree recovery, we are shifting our minds to think differently. The mind must think differently if we are going to enter the time we are living in and walk in victory and confidence. A transformed mind does not think like the world's blueprint (see Romans 12:1–2) but must redevelop a mindset of covenant. Worship in new ways. Do not grow comfortable!

This book is also about confrontation. Death and destruction are our enemies. Jane explains this war better than anyone I have known. War to enter the rest God has for you. Satan hates the thought of you multiplying and gaining control of resources he uses to hold us in captivity. Let a harvest mentality of increase develop in your mind. Leave the trauma of the past behind, and begin a new, fresh season of your life. Watch your emotions! Do not let past hurts and betrayals rule you. Receive revelation about your strongholds. Know what has held you captive in the past season. Let faith arise and increase, and express your faith with actions that will topple the thrones of iniquity! Receive the angelic hosts that will lead you into a new dimension of breakthrough! Catch the new wave of the Holy Spirit, and come alive and awaken to His best!

Let me say again that you were meant to prosper! Prosperity includes recovering what is lost and advancing into your destined future. The cares of this world are blinding. Loss, debt, and trauma structures can be overwhelming and prevent us from building and seeing clearly into the future. There is a law of recovery that is linked with the law of redemption. Naomi is a great example of demonstrating this in the Word of God. She had lost everything: her husband, her sons, and her place of prosperity in Bethlehem. She remembered the law of redemption and said, "I will return to Bethlehem and find my place again." Her daughter-in-law Ruth made covenant and accompanied her. The gates of Bethlehem welcomed them as they began to glean and recover. Ruth ended up marrying the wealthiest man in the city, and Naomi's inheritance was fully restored and recovered.

The Body of Christ needs to see restoration and recovery in our provision, for restoration is always linked with multiplication. Debt and past financial defeats in our lives need to reverse. Any spirit of poverty that has held our generational bloodlines in captivity and kept us from the fullness of the prosperity that

God has for us must be broken. The Lord is breaking the power of begging in His people. He is making us a people of faith. He will change the identity of His people from beggars to kings!

Believe that you can recover all and be restored!

Restoration is the power of returning to any place "God's best covenant plan was deviated from." Restoration includes reclaiming lost land, lost health, and lost joy. Restoration is linked with restitution. For instance, if a stone in your house was broken by a workman, it is substituted with another that is even better. I am declaring that every broken stone in your foundation will be replaced with new strength as you read this book. Restoration also means the perfecting, mending, or fitting together of every detail of your life that will cause you to complete or end your race greater than how you began it.

The enemy came to steal, kill, and destroy, but Yeshua came for you to enjoy life in abundance (see John 10:10)! If the enemy tried to overtake you in the past, I am decreeing that you will gain new strength to outrun him and finish stronger in your future. *Confronting the Thief* will empower you to war for your portion.

Dr. Chuck D. Pierce, president, Glory of Zion International
and Kingdom Harvest Alliance

INTRODUCTION

The thief does not come except to steal, and to kill, and to destroy. I have come that they may have life, and that they may have it more abundantly.

John 10:10

My husband, Tom, and I were on vacation recently in the south of France. We were wandering around a farmers market, going from stall to stall of fruits, vegetables, and flowers. I was wearing a cross-body purse on which I kept a firm hand. For a moment, however, I became distracted and reached for one of the products on display.

Suddenly someone brushed up against me and I felt my purse being unzipped. I grabbed it quickly and looked around. Two women were walking close beside me, acting as if nothing had happened. But before I knew it, a large man came up behind them and started screaming at them in French. He hit one woman in the head, and both took off running. The man ran after them, still screaming, obviously confronting them for trying to pick my pocket.

The thieves got away but were unsuccessful in taking my money. But how many times has the enemy picked our pockets and stolen from us while we were distracted by things happening around us?

Jesus warned us in John 10:10: "The thief's purpose is to steal and kill and destroy. My purpose is to give them a rich and satisfying life" (NLT). Clearly the thief is prowling around seeking to steal our finances, our health, our families, our peace, and our divine purpose. He seeks to kill our hopes and dreams. He is even determined to destroy the destiny of nations and generations.

As I prayed about this, I heard the Lord say, *The thieves did not succeed with you, nor will they succeed with My discerning* ekklesia [the Greek word for *church*, carrying the connotation of governing and ruling].[1] *I am opening your eyes to his tactics so you can identify his schemes. I am issuing a call to arms for My people, like the man who pursued the thieves, to discern the spirit of robbery, and, like David at Ziklag, to pursue, overtake, and recover all that's been stolen. It's time for My people to rise up and fight for their families and their land.*

We will look at the story of David at Ziklag (found in 1 Samuel 30) in chapter 7.

In the military sense, "a call to arms" is a summons by the government of a nation for its citizen army to report for active duty, to rise up and prepare for war. Similarly, we are living in a season of spiritual confrontation with our mortal enemy, the devil. God is issuing a challenge for the people of His Kingdom to hear the battle cry of the Spirit and to engage actively in the fight.

This is not a time to be passive spectators but active participants in the spiritual battle for our families, for our lives, and even for nations. A spiritual army is rising up and answering the call to confront the thief and take back all he has stolen. God is calling us out of casual, comfortable Christianity and enlisting us as volunteers in the army of the Lord. We have a real enemy, the devil, who is still active in the earth today. God's *ekklesia*, His called-out ones, His Church, is the primary restraining force against the devil's evil plans. We must engage in a tactical plan to recognize our enemy and resist his every move.

The Boxing Ring Vision

One Sunday several years ago, I had a vision of a boxing ring. Inside the ring were two demonic spirits named the Devourer and the Destroyer. They were not fighting each other but dancing around the ring, yelling at the assembled crowd and looking for an opponent. It was much like Goliath mocking and taunting Israel, saying, "Who is going to fight me?" These demons were jeering at the crowd of people, calling them cowards, mocking them and their Christ, and daring someone to step into the ring with them. They infuriated me!

As I looked at the crowd, I knew that most of the people were strong believers and leaders, but they seemed mesmerized by what was being said. No one moved. No one stepped up. This seemed unusual because these people were real fighters who never backed down when the enemy was present. As I watched, I wondered, *What's going on? Why doesn't someone get in the ring and knock their heads off and make them be quiet?* Then I saw the reason.

When boxers step into the ring, they often wear robes on their shoulders with their names written on the back. These demons had robes draped across their shoulders, but rather than their names, these words were written: *This is just life.*

Then I heard the voice of the Lord say, *Tell the people no! This is not "just life"! It's not "just life" that My people struggle financially during a bad economy. It's not "just life" when your children go into rebellion when they go to college. It's not "just life" when you get older and your body breaks down and you become vulnerable to sickness and disease. It is not "just life" that your nation is being swallowed up by wrong ideologies. These are the works of the Devourer and the Destroyer. Rise up and fight back in the Spirit and recover all they have stolen.*

I realized that the Lord was showing me that our enemy, the devil, is constantly finding ways to rob us. Sometimes we recognize that our challenging situations are works of darkness, but many other times we have just consigned ourselves to our loss, thinking, *Well, this is just life. This is just the way things go.*

While it is true we live in a fallen world that is not heaven on earth, there have probably been times in our lives when the Devourer and the Destroyer have robbed us without any consequence, simply because we did not recognize the act of robbery and we did not realize we had any recourse once the thief had struck.

The devil has been stealthily picking the pockets of the followers of Christ, robbing us unawares. Now is the time to recognize the thief, arrest him for his crime, and take back even more than he has taken from us! Lives are at stake. Families are in need of breakthrough. And nations hang in the balance, waiting for the people of God to rise up and fight back.

Divine Recovery

I have written this book after many years of prophetically discerning the activities of the thief and confronting his attacks on my own life and family, as well as on others in the Body of Christ.

In my book *Discernment: The Essential Guide to Hearing the Voice of God*, I relate a story about a local Christian couple who were very blessed in business, even during times of economic downturn. When I saw them at a community meeting, I heard the Spirit of the Lord say to me, *Go over there and break off the spirit of robbery.* I was shocked because they always seemed so blessed, but I crossed the room and told them what the Lord had said.

They told me that their real estate business had been under unusual attack over the past five weeks and had lost more than five million dollars' worth of contracts, each one right before closing. Although they had tried to analyze what had happened in each case, they could not figure out what they were doing wrong.

I told them it was not what they were doing wrong but that the thief, the spirit of robbery, was coming against them. I prayed over them, confronting the thief and declaring Exodus 22:7 over them: "If you catch a thief, he must restore double."

Five weeks later I received a phone call from this couple, saying that since I had prayed, their business had closed more than eleven million dollars' worth of contracts. God had indeed restored double of all the enemy had stolen.[2]

This is an example to me of divine recovery—God restoring all the enemy had stolen, and then some!

In my book *Declarations for Breakthrough: Agreeing with the Voice of God*, I relate another story in which the thief was identified and confronted. A couple in our church had a business installing a certain technology into our Florida schools and were operating on a $1.5 million annual grant from the state. When the economy went through a challenging season, however, they lost the funding.

That Sunday was the day I had the vision of the boxing ring, and I asked our congregation to repent of any "this is just life" mentalities in which the thief had robbed them and they had just accepted it. This couple, I learned later, looked at one another and realized, *We've been robbed!* So they repented of merely accepting it and determined to take back what had been stolen.

That week they filled out an application for re-funding for the project. They also wrote a decree for divine recovery of what had been stolen from them. A decree is an inspired statement of promise from the word of God, which one declares verbally or in writing, releasing victory over a situation (see Job 22:28). The next Sunday they brought both documents with them to church, as well as an offering to the Lord to see the devourer rebuked (see Malachi 3:10–11). We prayed over these documents before they resubmitted the application for funding.

In the next several weeks, not only was their funding restored, but they were told that their project was never supposed to have been defunded in the first place. Our governor's office told them they would receive last year's funding of $1.5 million, plus the state was going to double the current year's funding to $3 million—a double-portion restoration of all the thief had stolen from them.

It did not end there. Over the next several weeks, their annual funding for this project went from $3 million to $9 million to $17 million to $25 million—an exponential divine recovery of what had been stolen from them. They went from near bankruptcy to incredible prosperity because they had broken the lie of the robber and taken back all he had stolen. Additionally, they opened the way for this project to be funded on a national level.[3]

This is divine recovery! It was not just what they could do for themselves in the natural realm by following good principles; it was supernatural intervention in their lives and business, enabling them to fulfill all God had called them to accomplish through this project.

Exposing the Robbers

One night I was awakened by the Spirit of the Lord speaking these words to me: *It is time for the hanging of Haman's ten sons.*

I researched this in the book of Esther about the battle against the wicked Haman, the enemy of the Jews. I began to understand that Esther is not a Cinderella story about an orphan girl who became queen. Rather, this is a story about the modern-day Church, the *ekklesia*, who like Esther is coming from obscurity, answering the call of God, purifying her heart, determining to love not her life unto the death, and going into the throne room of the King in righteous intercession. The Church, like Esther, is being asked to confront the enemy's assignment of death and destruction, to overturn the decrees of the enemy, and to break the power of the spirit of robbery that wants to take not only our lives but our peace, our power, and our prophetic promise, just as Haman tried to do in this story from long ago.

The Bible calls Haman an Agagite. Agag was the king of the Amalekite tribe (see 1 Samuel 15:8). One meaning of the name *Amalekite* is "blood licker,"[4] as they were fierce opponents in battle. They were a tribe of raiders and plunderers of unsuspecting travelers[5] and can be characterized as possessing the spirit of robbery, for each time we find them in Scripture, they are robbing Israel and conspiring with her enemies. The Bible says of Saul, when he was establishing his rule, that "he gathered an army and attacked the Amalekites, and delivered Israel from the hands of those who plundered them" (1 Samuel 14:48). The word *plunder* means to rob or to spoil.[6]

According to Genesis 36:12, Amalek's mother was Timna, which means restraint, derived from the Hebrew *mana*, meaning to deny, to withhold, or to keep back;[7] and his father was Eliphaz, which means "god of gold."[8] This is a spiritual enemy that attempts to keep believers from their destiny in Christ, to restrain them from fulfilling vision, and to prevent them from accessing God's provision for their lives.

The Amalekites warred against Israel at important moments in history and tried to thwart her advancement at every turn. They were the first warring tribe that Israel fought with after the Red Sea victory over Pharaoh. They were the tribe that stood in the way and hindered Israel from answering God's call to possess the land. It was an Amalekite who claimed to have dealt the death blow to King Saul on the battlefield—who, though a reprobate, was still considered by David to be God's anointed one. The Amalekites plundered the crops in the days of Gideon, and robbed David's camp at Ziklag, capturing not only possessions but family members as well.

Because of their assignment to rob and oppress God's people, and because of the injustice they measured out, God said He would "have war with Amalek from generation to generation" (Exodus 17:16). This tribe is an Old Testament personification of the thief Jesus warned us about.

This book will demonstrate the ways the enemy comes to rob us, just as the Amalekites tried to rob and defeat the people of God in Israel's history. It will continue through the story of Esther and the ultimate victory over this enemy tribe.

In the story of Esther, Haman and his ten sons were all killed, ending the natural lineage of the Amalekites. Each of Haman's sons' names has a Persian meaning that indicates ways in which the enemy tries to rob individuals, families, and even nations of their destiny. Toward the end of this book, we will explore the meanings of each of these ten names and make decrees against their power.

The spirit of robbery continues to torment and harass God's people today. In understanding its tactics, we can arise in wisdom, strength, and revelation, not only to conquer a foe, but also to defeat our own flesh and our own fear, living in victory through Christ every day. This victory will empower us to triumph and recover all he has stolen from us.

I would like you to make this bold decree over your life and family as we begin our journey together. Please say it out loud and with authority as Psalm 81:10 declares: "Open your mouth with a mighty decree; I will fulfill it now, you'll see! The words that you speak, so shall it be!" (TPT).

YOUR DECREE OF VICTORY

[Speak this aloud in faith!] *I decree that I will see recovery in every area the thief has robbed from me, my family, my church, and my nation. I repent of every attitude that has put the enemy's robbery into a "this is just life" category in my mind, producing a sense of helplessness, hopelessness, and passivity. I decree, by the power of the Holy Spirit living in me, that I will answer God's call to arms against this enemy and become part of the army of the Lord called to push back evil in my time. I will receive tactical strategies to identify and confront the thief. I will take back everything that has been stolen from me. And I will see a full manifestation of divine recovery—a supernatural turnaround in every area of my life. In Jesus' mighty name.*

PRAY WITH ME

Lord, I pray that You will open my eyes that I might see every area the enemy has committed robbery against me. Give me spiritual discernment to see how this may have affected me or those I love. I ask Your Holy Spirit to enlighten my heart as I read this book that I might experience the fullness of divine recovery and abundant life, as You have promised. In Jesus' name. Amen.

QUESTIONS TO CONSIDER

1. What are some areas that come to your mind when considering what the enemy may have robbed from you?

2. Do you feel you were aware of the possibility that these losses were due to some spiritual force, or do you feel you categorized the loss as "this is just life"?

3. Are you willing to change the way you think of these situations and answer God's call to arms to engage in spiritual battle for divine recovery?

4. What would you need to do differently to engage in battle?

5. What would recovery look like for you?

ONE

DIVINE RECOVERY

A thief has only one thing in mind—he wants to steal, slaughter, and destroy. But I have come to give you everything in abundance, more than you expect—life in its fullness until you overflow!

John 10:10 TPT

James and Monika had a prosperous internet-based business run by Kingdom principles. They were diligent to listen to the voice of God regarding their tithe and additional giving. As a matter of fact, one year the Lord instructed them to tithe a specific amount each week, which would represent increase over the previous year's income. He also instructed them to give sizable offerings at specific times during the upcoming year.

In April of that year, however, God spoke to them that shaking was coming to their business, even though things seemed to be going well. In May they suffered a devastating cyberattack on their data center. All website content and business connections were being held for ransom, and the data center decided it would not pay. All content was completely lost. Everything they had worked seven years to establish was stolen from them instantly. There seemed to be nothing they could do to fix it except pray.

I had the opportunity to pray with James and Monika, to break the assignment of the thief and to declare divine recovery over all that was theirs. Some of the large offerings the Lord told them to give were designated for the month of May. They sowed them in obedience even though it looked as if all hope was lost with their business. God spoke to them and said, *Give, and see what I will do.*

This is when God began to show off. Miracles began happening for them day after day. The year before, they had moved their business from another state and applied for certification in the state of Florida. Their business application had been declined. But now, a year later, after giving, they were notified that their business was approved for registration in Florida, even though they had never reapplied. Even the activation fee of $400 was somehow paid in full.

Additionally, a website company was able to retrieve most of the content from their lost website, alleviating the need to rewrite everything for the new website. They were able to launch a new temporary website within two weeks, which allowed Google to start reestablishing their business rankings—extremely important for online businesses.

Miraculously, sales started pouring in from long-forgotten accounts and random connections with customers, which helped them remain afloat financially during the rebuilding time.

Their new website was launched by the end of August. But just as they were gaining momentum, there was one more setback for their company. Google removed all their business reviews and page rankings because they had violated some unwritten code by offering prayers with their business emails.

Rather than just sit back and take everything the enemy was dishing out, James and Monika decided to fight back. They took their prophetic words and promises from the Word of God and wrote two pages of decrees over their business, speaking them out loud together daily. They also brought these to my husband, Tom, and me to pray over, declaring once again that they would experience divine recovery over all their losses.

By the beginning of October, their business was down forty percent from the previous year. This challenged their faith walk. But by December 31, they found that not only had they fully recovered from their deficit, but their company had increased fifteen percent over the previous year. In the last two months of the year, they did more business than in all the previous months put together.

This is what it looks like when we confront the thief and declare divine recovery over our lives, our businesses, and our families.

Jesus' Mission: Divine Recovery

Jesus' mission in the earth was to expose and overthrow the thief, and at the same time give His followers a life of blessing and overflow. He came to restore mankind to right relationship with the Father; and beyond saving our souls from hell, He came to redeem us, restore us, and recover all that the enemy has stolen from us. This is what the Gospel of the Kingdom looks like.

The word used in John 10:10 for the "abundant" life Jesus came to give is the Greek word *perissos*, which means beyond, superabundant (in quantity), superior (in quality), beyond measure,[1] or extraordinary.[2] The thief comes to rob you of both the quality of your life and the quantity of your blessings. Jesus is telling us that He came to earth to give us a life of abundance in every area beyond measure. The life of the believer is to be superior in quality and extraordinary in every way.

Jesus was God in flesh, sent as God's ambassador of divine recovery to the world He loves, defeating the thief and restoring us to abundant life. This is not about money or possessions, but about living lives of purpose, freedom, joy, and victory.

For those in bondage to sin, Jesus came to recover freedom, wholeness, and life. For those ravaged by sickness and disease, He came to recover health and strength. For those living in poverty and lack, He promises abundance and supernatural provision. For those oppressed by the devil, He promises lives of peace, power, and liberty.

The American Heritage Dictionary defines the word *recover*:

> To get back (something lost or taken away) . . . to search for, find, and bring back . . . to get back control or possession of (land) by military conquest or legal action; to have (the use, possession, or control of something) restored . . . to regain the use of (a faculty) or be restored to (a normal or usual condition) . . . to receive a favorable judgment in a lawsuit.[3]

These definitions give us an idea of what God desires to do in activating and authorizing believers everywhere to operate in the authority of Christ to subdue Satan and recover all he has stolen. When we experience divine recovery, God enables us to return to a previous position of peace and prosperity in our lives and demonstrate a great personal comeback story.

To further clarify and emphasize the concept of recovery, following are some of the synonyms that express the broad scope of application of this term, according to *Webster's New World Thesaurus*: "the act of regaining possession, restoration, reformation, revival, reawakening, recuperation, resurrection, resurgence, rejuvenation, renewal, recapture, rally, redemption and reclamation."[4] Wow! This is what I want my life and spiritual journey to look like. How about you?

I realize these are a lot of words, but I love definitions. I love the depth of understanding they provide in breaking down and analyzing a prophetic concept.

Think about it: When we experience divine recovery, God turns things for the better. He restores our souls and gives us back "the years that the swarming locust has eaten" (Joel 2:25). He gives us the courage to reclaim what has been stolen. We regain prosperity, health, joy, vision, and life. He gives us the power to rally in the midst of trying times. He releases healing, recuperation, provision—and, yes, even revival! He empowers us to overcome difficulties so we can become freedom-makers and world-shakers. When the Church experiences the anointing of divine recovery and utilizes the power Jesus released to us, we can turn the world upside down!

Recovery in the Court of Heaven

One of the dictionary definitions of *recovery* is "to receive a favorable judgment in a lawsuit." Do you realize there is a court in heaven where God, the great Judge, makes decisions on behalf of His people?

The prophet Daniel gives us a view of these heavenly court proceedings: "I watched as thrones were put in place and the Ancient One sat down to judge. . . . Then the court began its session, and the books were opened" (Daniel 7:9–10 NLT). Verse 22 goes on to say that, when the enemy seemed to be prevailing, the Ancient of Days made a court decision "in favor of his holy people" (NLT), and they took over the Kingdom.

We need to understand our position in God's heavenly courtroom and that judgments are being made in our favor. We recognize the devil as a thief, a criminal, who has stolen from

God's people and killed not only bodies but hopes and dreams, destroying many lives. He has stolen property, opportunities, health, children, and destinies. The devil has even sought to disempower the people of God within a territory or nation so he can steal righteousness and spiritual life, pulling lands into darkness through corruption, iniquity, and idolatry.

It is beneficial, therefore, to understand the legal application of the term *recovery* as it pertains to judgments in courts of law here on earth, so we can apply the same principles to the court in heaven and bring our mortal enemy to justice. When something has been stolen, one can bring suit in a court of law and receive a formal legal judgment or vindication and have the stolen right or property restored.

Once again, in terms a layperson can more readily understand, recovery is getting back what belongs to us. When the enemy steals from us, not only is he obligated to give back what he has taken, but he must pay back even more in "damages." It is our job to enforce the victory Christ has already given us and make the devil pay.

I heard a minister say once that whenever there was a murder or violent crime in his city, he would assemble a team, go to the site of the crime, and share the Gospel until several people were saved. He was determined to make the devil pay in souls for crimes committed against his city.

Replevin from Heaven

When a dear friend and fellow minister, Alex Florence from Edmonton, Alberta, Canada, was praying and seeking the Lord a number of years ago, he saw a vision of a word forming in the air in front of him. It read *R-E-P-L-E-V-I-N*. He had no idea what this word meant so he grabbed a dictionary and looked it up.

Replevin, it turns out, is a legal term used by judges, a procedure to help a person take back property that has been wrongfully taken. My friend Alex realized that the Lord was speaking to him in spiritual terms to have God, the great Judge, issue a legal "Writ of Replevin" from heaven, authorizing believers to take back everything the enemy had stolen from them. Alex was receiving this legal action straight from the court of heaven, with all the ramifications of recovering stolen property. As he has shared this publicly, it has activated divine recovery for many.

In a secular court of law, there is a procedure to file for a Writ of Replevin:

1. Prepare a complaint by compiling a list of what has been taken.

2. Prepare a replevin summons, a notice for the defendant to appear in court. This is done spiritually through prayer, fasting, preparing for a confrontation, and perhaps even writing a decree over your situation. Job 22:28 (NASB1995) says, "You will also decree a thing, and it will be established for you; and light will shine on your ways." Decrees are powerful and legal spiritual tools used not only to confront the enemy, but to state your position.

3. File documents with the court requesting a return of property. Isaiah 43:25–26 says, "I, even I, am He who blots out your transgressions for My own sake; and I will not remember your sins." It is important to repent if we have contributed to our loss through sin, carelessness, or lack of discernment. God goes on to say, "Put Me in remembrance; let us contend together; state your case, that you may be acquitted" (verse 26). The only way we can be acquitted is through the power of the

blood of Jesus Christ, which makes us worthy to approach God's throne. But God invites us to "put Him in remembrance." We remind the Lord of His promises and prophetic words over our lives as we state our case before Him.

4. Await the Writ of Replevin after the hearing, when the judge enters his judgment. In heaven's courtroom, we deal with the accuser and thief and then await the judgment in our favor from our Judge and King. Colossians 2:14 says that God "canceled the certificate of debt consisting of decrees against us, which was hostile to us; and He has taken it out of the way, having nailed it to the cross" (NASB). By the cross of Christ, we have access, favor, and the right to see every decree of robbery written against us overturned.

5. Take the Writ of Replevin, authorizing the individual to demand the return of his or her property, to local law enforcement for assistance in getting the property back. Although the government will back up the demand, it is the responsibility of the individual to serve the Writ of Replevin upon the thief and get his or her property back. Going through this process can involve time and money, but it can result in the recovery of all that has been taken.[5] Just as God spoke to David when he and his men were robbed at Ziklag, we, too, must "pursue, for you shall surely overtake them and without fail recover all" (1 Samuel 30:8).

Likewise, when the enemy steals from believers, we need to realize that we have recourse. We are not helpless or hopeless but must be willing to contend for recovery. It may take time and effort, but we must recognize that the devil is a legalist.

Although Jesus Christ has broken his power here on earth, it is up to us to enforce that victory. So whether through prayers, decrees, or even prophetic acts, file your complaint of replevin. Describe all that has been stolen, and include damages for lost joy, stolen peace, pain and suffering, and the like. Then approach the court of heaven and request your Writ of Replevin. Psalm 149:6–9 tells us:

> Let the high praises of God be in their mouth, and a two-edged sword in their hand, to execute vengeance on the nations, and punishments on the peoples; to bind their kings with chains, and their nobles with fetters of iron; to execute on them the written judgment—this honor have all His saints. Praise the LORD!

Believers have been given the honor of executing and enforcing the legal judgments written from heaven's court here in the earth.

Throne Room Litigation

Jesus told His disciples in John 14:16 that He was getting ready to leave them but that He would pray for the Father to send them another Comforter, "that he may abide with you for ever" (KJV). The word for *Comforter* is the Greek word *parakletos*. One of the meanings of *parakletos* is the concept of advocate[6] or defense attorney, one who pleads another's case before a judge; counsel for defense; an intercessor.[7]

The Holy Spirit is our *parakletos*, our defense attorney, our Advocate in the court of heaven. The blood of Jesus makes atonement for our sin, exposes the lies of our accuser, and defends us against all unjust attacks. This gives us authority to overturn the decrees and legal judgments the thief has made against us and our families, and enables us to bring him to justice.

In the times of kings, legal matters were brought before the king to decide matters. Our King also happens to be the great Judge, who through the blood of His Son has already declared our innocence, freedom, and restoration.

Hebrews 4:16 paints a picture regarding our access to the heavenly throne room, where our litigation takes place. This verse urges us to "come boldly to the throne of grace, that we may obtain mercy and find grace to help in time of need." The beauty of this picture is that it is a throne of grace, meaning that we may have been guilty of sin, carelessness, or ignorance, yet He forgives and fully restores when we approach His throne with repentance and confession. Because of His grace, we can come boldly before the throne of the King.

The word *boldly* is the Greek word *parrhesia*, which means with outspokenness, frankness, bluntness, or assurance and confidence.[8] *Thayer's Greek-English Lexicon* defines this word as "to come with freedom in speaking, unreservedness in speech, open, honest and even blunt speech. To come with free and fearless confidence in a cheerful and courageous manner."[9] This is how our King wants us to approach Him. It does not mean we should be disrespectful of Him or His position in any way; even so, we come as heirs, not as criminals or commoners, knowing that He hears us. It is there we obtain mercy (*eleos*, compassion[10] and kindness[11]) for our situation and find grace to help in our time of need.

In the second volume of his book *Sparkling Gems from the Greek*, Rick Renner brings a whole different perspective on Hebrews 4:16 and on receiving help in time of need:

> The phrase is a translation of the Greek word *boetheia*, a word with a military connotation. The word *boetheia* can be translated to help, as to help a person with his or her needs, but the

military connotation of this word adds much more meaning and makes it really powerful. . . .

[It] depicted the exact moment when a soldier heard that his fellow fighter was entrenched in battle, captured, or struggling. Once alerted to this situation, the soldier quickly went into battle to fight for the safety and well-being of his fellow fighter. For that soldier, just hearing of a fellow fighter in need was all that was necessary to beckon him into battle. He spared no effort to deliver his brother as he went into action to rescue him and bring him back into a place of safety, security, and protection.

The Holy Spirit uses this same word to tell us that when we get into trouble and we tell Jesus about it, He goes into battle like a Mighty Warrior to be our defense and to secure our deliverance!

When Jesus fights, He is always on the winning side.[12]

So we see that when we come boldly before God's throne of grace, not only does it activate a legal claim in the courts of heaven, but Jesus, our mighty Man of War, rises up to secure our deliverance.

Similarly, when we understand our legal position with our King and Judge, it opens the door for our intercession for others. The Greek word for "obtaining mercy" carries a connotation of having goodwill toward others who are miserable or afflicted; it stirs in us a desire to help them.[13] When we search out and discover the depths of God's grace, it should challenge us to press into His Word to discover our legal rights as citizens of the Kingdom of God for the benefit of ourselves, our families, and others. Our place before the throne should never be only for ourselves but to lift the cause of others as well. This is intercession.

So legally in the court of heaven, in the throne room of the King, we are given grace to cover all our sins or mistakes so we can make our petition confidently and courageously, and state the case for recovery for ourselves and for others. As we read the Word of God, we investigate our legal rights as believers and discover Scriptures we can stand on to present our case.

As we do, God mobilizes the heavenly host in a call to battle to help those who are being oppressed, harassed, or robbed by the enemy. He becomes "a very present help in trouble" (Psalm 46:1). He arises not just as King or Judge but also as the mighty Man of War who fights for us. And He is on time—every single time!

Replevin Manifested

After the revelation of "replevin from heaven" that Alex Florence shared with us, I began to share it with others, declaring that we can take back whatever has been lost, stolen, or even hidden from us. I soon began to hear of miracles of recovery from friends, family, and church members.

One woman in our church began to declare replevin over her life, family, and finances. Within a short time, she received an unexpected check in the mail for over $8,000 from a company she had worked for more than twenty years before. Apparently there had been some sort of employee savings plan withheld from her paycheck, which was never returned when she left. Her declarations of replevin seemed to spark a review of records in the heavens as well as within the company, which returned long-forgotten money.

One woman saw one of her prodigal children return to the Lord and break free of addiction. Another woman received healing in one of her eyes that had been damaged by a virus. Doctors told her the loss of vision was permanent; but as she contended for replevin (or recovery), God restored her eyesight completely and miraculously! Another woman reported having a $30,000 medical bill forgiven. A man reported he had more than $40,000 in credit card debt forgiven. A couple had a $56,000 debt due to a legal matter erased.

Miracles, it seemed, were breaking out all over. Prodigals returned home, families were reconciled, legal matters were settled in favor of the believers, and healings and miracles began to take place—all because believers realized they were not helpless in dealing with matters in which the enemy seemed to have taken advantage of them. When they began to rise up with authority to declare God's Word of recovery and restoration to their personal situations, things suddenly shifted.

Appeal to Heaven

Some years ago the prophetic leader Dutch Sheets received a revelation, through a series of dreams of some friends, regarding the very first flag of the United States. On this flag, which actually predated the Stars and Stripes, is a picture of a pine tree (a symbol of covenant) and the words *An Appeal to Heaven*, written boldly on a white background. This phrase was written by British philosopher John Locke in his work *Two Treatises of Government*. Locke was addressing the issues of robbery and injustice in the natural realm, which finds a remedy in appealing to heaven:

> What is my Remedy against a Robber, that so broke into my House? Appeal to the Law for Justice. But perhaps Justice is denied, or I am crippled and cannot stir, robbed and have not the means to do it. . . . But the Conquered, or their Children, have no court, no Arbitrator on Earth to appeal to. Then they may appeal, as Jephtha did, to Heaven, and repeat their Appeal, till they have recovered the native Right of their Ancestors, which was to have such a Legislative over them.[14]

Locke went on:

> And where the body of the people, or any single man, is deprived of their right, or is under the exercise of a power without

right, and have no appeal on earth, then they have a liberty to appeal to heaven.[15]

In other words, when human justice fails you, when you have been robbed and no one is held accountable, when your appeals for restitution have seemingly fallen on deaf ears, you have the right to make an appeal to heaven to find justice, breakthrough, and divine recovery.

The Shunammite's Victory

We read a biblical depiction of the appeal to heaven in 2 Kings 8 in the story of the woman from Shunem who wanted to recover her house and her land. This is the same woman who received a miracle through the prophet Elisha, bearing a son after many years of barrenness. Not only did she experience a miracle pregnancy, but when the boy was a teen and fell over dead, this Shunammite woman, full of faith, appealed to the prophet and saw her son raised from the dead.

Several chapters later Elisha told the Shunammite that there would be a famine in the land for seven years and that she and her family should go live somewhere else. She did. But during that time, someone else moved into her house and took posses-sion of her land. To be clear, it belonged to her. But when she obeyed the prophet, a robber saw an opportunity and took it.

She could just have said, "Oh well, this is life! After all, I was gone for seven years." No! She did not accept the "this is just life" lie. She had not accepted it when her son dropped dead years before, and she would not accept it now. Recognizing that she had been robbed, the Shunammite "went to make an appeal to the king for her house and for her land" (2 Kings 8:3). She went to the throne room of the king asking for justice.

That day she was probably just one among many waiting to make her appeal to the king. But as she waited, the king was having a conversation with the servant of Elisha, Gehazi. The king wanted to hear about the great deeds of Elisha. And as the servant told the story of the woman whose son Elisha had restored back to life, he looked up and saw the very woman and her son, waiting to speak with the king!

> And Gehazi said, "My lord, O king, this is the woman, and this is her son whom Elisha restored to life." And when the king asked the woman, she told him. So the king appointed a certain officer for her, saying, "Restore all that was hers, and all the proceeds of the field from the day that she left the land until now."
>
> 2 Kings 8:5–6

The Shunammite experienced a *kairos* moment—just the right time!—as she came before the throne to find help in her time of need. Notice, she had made an appeal for both her house and her land. And she was in the right place at the right time to receive the king's favor and to be granted her request for recovery.

This is the position of the *ekklesia* today. We need to contend for our own houses, our own needs, our own families, our own places of personal breakthrough—and we also need to contend for our land, our territory, and our nation. It is not an either-or situation; it is both-and. We need to rise up, shake off the grief and trauma of having been robbed, and make our appeal to the King—an appeal to heaven for full recovery.

The king's decree to the Shunammite was to restore all. The word *restore* is the Hebrew word *shuwb*, which means to turn back, to recompense, to recover.[16] The Shunammite was not just going to get back her house and land, which had been stolen, but she was to receive full recovery of all the fruit of the land, which should have been hers, from the time she left the land until that day. And to make sure she got back all that was hers, and all that should have been hers, the king appointed "a certain officer" of the court to assist her and to enforce the restoration.

This, I believe, is the picture of God sending angelic hosts from His throne room to enforce the Writ of Replevin issued from His court. Now that is divine recovery!

Shalam!

My dear friend Robert Gay sets an expectation for divine recovery through a marvelous testimony in his book *Voices: Hearing and Discerning When God Speaks*. He writes:

> On October 10, 2018, Hurricane Michael, a Category 5 tropical cyclone, hit the panhandle of Florida. The eye of the storm that packed 165 mph winds and gusts near 200 mph went directly over the eastern part of Bay County, Florida. It just so happened that the eye of the storm passed straight over my home and the church building where I pastor. Our entire area was devastated. It looked as if an atomic bomb had exploded and leveled most things in a radius of 20 miles or more. It was terrifying and heartbreaking.
>
> My wife and our family evacuated during the storm and retreated to Orlando. During the storm, we watched on television as it traveled its path. A category five hurricane causes catastrophic damage (only four category five storms have ever hit the US since 1851). So, all we could do was pray, wait, and believe for the best.
>
> When pictures came back of the sheer devastation, the Lord gave me a prophetic word for our congregation and the people of the area. The Lord spoke to me the scripture found in Joel 2:25, "I will restore to you . . ." I shared the word in a video

on Facebook and encouraged our people. I still have very vivid memories of that moment. . . .

Later, I did a word study specifically on the word "restore," which is the Hebrew word shalam. This word is the root word for shalom. When the word shalam is used and translated as "restore," it typically means to have a greater amount than you had previously, more than you had before. This was quickened to me by the Lord, and I started declaring that we would have more than we had before. Our entire church body started using the word "shalam" and saying that we would have more than we had before.

As time went by, there were testimonies of people who received large settlements and payouts that resulted in their homes ending up in a better condition than before the hurricane. The testimonies poured in from people concerning restoration of their properties. Their situations on the other side of the storm were better than before the devastation. Many companies and private contractors made more financially than they had in the history of their businesses.

God fulfilled His Word; He did what He said He would do. Our church was not only able to repair and restore the damage, but we were able to eliminate the remaining debt on the building. I was able to repair the damage to my home and have funds left over for improvements. God did exactly what He said, and we had more than we had before. Hallelujah! His Word brought forth a resurrection. His Word caused the dry bones to live.[17]

Thank you, Robert, for these encouraging words!

A PROPHETIC WORD FOR YOU

I hear the Lord saying to you: *This is a season I am declaring* shalam *over your life—more than before and better than before. I am opening up your eyes to the ways the enemy has tried to bring destruction in your life and family, that you might con-tend with Me, state your case, and see things turn around. You are not helpless or hopeless, so make your appeal for your house and your land. Though you have been wearied in the battle, I am releasing new strength for you to confront the enemy. I am issuing a decree of favor from My throne over your life and circumstances. Come to Me and detail all that has been lost and watch Me turn things for your good. This is your season to recover all.*

YOUR DECREE FOR DIVINE RECOVERY

[Speak this aloud in faith!] *This is my time for divine recov-ery and replevin from heaven. As I approach God's throne of grace, I will find mercy and help in my time of need. The Lord is my Judge and King and is ruling in my favor. I repent of every sin, as well as my presumption, lack of faith, and failure to listen to God's voice, which may have contributed to my circumstances. I receive full acquittal by the blood of Jesus and receive favor from God's throne. Thank You, Lord, for restoring more than before and even better than before in my life. I receive the* shalam *anointing and declare that all that the enemy has stolen is being fully recompensed. I declare Joel 2:25 over my life, that You, Lord, will restore to me all the locust has eaten or destroyed, including my years of loss. I will eat in plenty and be satisfied and praise the name of the Lord. In Jesus' mighty name.*

QUESTIONS TO CONSIDER

1. How would your life look different if you were experi-encing the abundant life Jesus came to bring—superior

in quality and extraordinary? Write a description of what would need to change.

2. When you consider coming into God's throne room, have you ever felt you could not be free or honest with Him about your need for mercy and grace? Why do you think this is? Remember, He has given you permission to be bold, cheerful, and courageous as you approach Him. Take time now to share your needs honestly and openly with Him.

3. What are some issues you need to bring into the court of heaven to make your appeal? File your Writ of Replevin before God's heavenly throne.

4. Just as the Shunammite appealed to the king for her house and land, what petitions do you need to make to see divine recovery in your own house? What petitions are you appealing to heaven for in your land (church, community, city, or nation)?

5. In what areas of your life do you want to experience the *shalam* anointing for recovery? Write this into your own decree.

TWO

POSSESSING OUR PROMISE

Be sober-minded; be watchful. Your adversary the devil prowls around like a roaring lion, seeking someone to devour.

1 Peter 5:8 ESV

An intercessor friend, Brenda Johnson, had a dream in which she and her husband were being robbed. In the dream they heard the thieves downstairs, so they ran down to confront them. There were two of them, a man and a woman. Quickly they laid hold of these thieves and demanded, "Why are you robbing us?" One thief replied with an evil smile, "Because I can." It was as if the thief were saying, "Who's going to stop us?"

The devil is a thief and a liar. His best strategy is to convince believers that we are helpless against his attacks. He tries to convince us that there is nothing we can do to stop him from harassing, tormenting, and robbing the righteous. He traps us in sin, afflicts our bodies with sickness and disease, and arrests our minds with oppression and fear. If he can convince believers that we are vulnerable and lack the authority to confront him, he will continue working his demonic tricks unhindered.

But this is exactly why Jesus came to earth. First John 3:8 tells us, "For this purpose the Son of God was manifested, that He might destroy the works of the devil." *The Passion Translation* says it this way: "The reason the Son of God was revealed was to undo and destroy the works of the devil." Everything Jesus did was to destroy the works of hell in the earth and to bring His people into full restoration and recovery of all that was lost. Jesus came to destroy every curse, break every chain of bondage, and completely revoke all power and authority from the devil.

Not only that, but Jesus came to give us abundant life superior in quality and superabundant in quantity—extraordinary! In *Thayer's Greek-English Lexicon*, the Greek word for *abundant* means over and above, more than necessary, even "superadded."[1] Wow! Jesus came not only to expose and destroy all the works of the devil but to turn around and bring an exceedingly abundant divine recovery of everything the devil has stolen—more than was lost, more than is necessary.

Second Timothy 1:10 in *The Passion Translation* tells us that Jesus is "our life-giver, who has dismantled death, obliterating all its effects on our lives, and has manifested his immortal life in us by the gospel." He is the One who gives us hope, life, and freedom, and not just a little bit! He wants to give us life that overflows with His goodness and mercy.

An Extravagant God

Jesus' intention when He came to earth was to show the heart of the Father to lost humanity. Everything He did demonstrated God's superabundant love and grace, removing the chasm sin had created and making a way for reconciliation between God and mankind. There were times Jesus healed individuals, and times He healed entire crowds. He extended His invitation of love and life to religious leaders and prostitutes alike. He was no respecter of who the person was or what he or she had done. Jesus loved them just the same and longed to demonstrate God's goodness to them.

One day He spoke to two fishermen who had been out fishing all night and caught nothing. He told them to push back out into the deep water and let down their nets, and this time they would catch something. These were seasoned fishermen who could have argued that Jesus was no fisherman and did not know what He was talking about, and that this was not the way these things worked. Instead Simon responded, "If You say so, we will do it." Suddenly their nets were swamped with a huge haul of fish that threatened to sink their boat, straining the nets past their capacity. There were so many fish they had to signal to other fishermen in another boat to come help them pull in their catch. (Read the story in Luke 5:4–11.)

Jesus demonstrated abundant life to Simon and his companions that day. They did not just pull in enough fish to feed their families; they pulled in two boatloads of fish, enough to set them up financially for the season. But they were so overwhelmed by His extravagant goodness that the fishermen left their boats and nets and immediately followed Christ. Jesus said they would no longer be fishing for fish: "From now on you will catch men" (verse 10).

On another occasion Jesus had been traveling around with His disciples doing miracles, teaching, and casting demons out of the oppressed. After a long day, He had drawn a crowd of more than five thousand men, besides women and children. Who knows how many thousands were following Jesus that day, listening to Him teach and seeing the healings He performed?

As the day wore on, the disciples brought a very natural problem into this supernatural scenario. They were in a remote place with nowhere for the people to buy food. The disciples' solution? Send the people away so they could travel to one of the surrounding villages before it got too late. Jesus had a different solution: "You guys give them something to eat."

I can only imagine the looks on the disciples' faces. There were thousands of hungry people, and all the disciples could find was five loaves of bread and two fish. What was Jesus thinking?

But Jesus said, "Bring those to Me." He had everyone sit down on the grass. Then He blessed the food and had the disciples hand it out. The food was multiplied right before their eyes. When it was all over, everyone had eaten not just a morsel or a mouthful, but their fill, until they were satisfied; and now there were twelve baskets left over. They went from complete lack to leftovers! (Read the story in Matthew 14:13–21.)

Jesus was proving a point. He was demonstrating abundant life, showing them that His Father was a God of extravagance. God did not want to barely bless them with enough to get by, but with more than enough to satisfy their needs. Jesus was showing them that God did not just want to save their souls from hell; His desire was for them to live healed in their bodies and minds, free and happy in their hearts, and with abundant supply in their provisions, the way He originally intended. These miracles of Jesus were God's invitation to the people to have a relationship with a loving, giving, unlimited Father.

One of the covenantal names of God is *El Shaddai*, God almighty, the all-sufficient God, or even the God who is more than enough.[2] Jesus came to demonstrate the character and nature of God to a fallen world. He lacks nothing. He is more than enough.

The religious Pharisees of the day had painted an entirely different picture of God. He was hard, stern, and angry with the people. Jesus showed them, by contrast, that while God is righteous and holy, He is also a loving Father who delights in blessing His children. Jesus came to offer us freedom from sin and shame and to give us direct access to the very heart of God.

Some say that Jesus was demonstrating the God of grace and mercy, love and kindness—the "New Testament God"—whereas the "Old Testament God" was harsh and severe. But the truth is, in both Old and New Testaments, He is the same God. He has always looked for ways to have a relationship with His people and to bless them. Jesus said in Luke 12:32, "Do not fear, little flock, for it is your Father's good pleasure to give you the kingdom."

Possessing Our Promised Land

We see God's nature of abundance and extravagance pictured in the land promised to Israel coming out of Egyptian captivity. That land looked different in those days compared to the barren land much of it is today.

The Promised Land was described as good and spacious, flowing with milk and honey. Ezekiel called it the most glorious of all lands (see Ezekiel 20:6; Exodus 3:8; Numbers 14:8). This emphasized the fertility of the soil and the lush vegetation that awaited God's people. The flowing milk was an indication that flocks could find pasture in the rich farmland, and it would be a land of fertility to raise families. The dripping honey is a picture of beautiful fields of flowers and varieties of plants where bees could draw nectar. It was a promise that the years of bitterness, bondage, and barrenness in Egypt would be behind them, and they could thrive and prosper as a people in their own land, a land of delight, pleasure, and plenty.

44

This was God's heart for Israel, His chosen people. He delighted in bringing them out of captivity and into a place of promise. Sure, there were tribes in the land, including giants, that would need to be driven out. They had been the caretakers of the land until Israel would arrive. But God clearly stated that, once the sin of the current inhabitants was "complete" (Genesis 15:16), He was giving this land to His people, and that they should cross over right away and possess it.

Have you ever wondered why God makes promises to us? He is the Creator of the universe, after all, the sovereign Lord. He does not owe us that. Yet He gives us promises from His Word for our families, our health, our prosperity, and our future. He is the promise-maker and the promise-keeper. He gives prophetic dreams, visions, and promises regarding what He desires to accomplish in and through us. Normally He paints a picture for us, much as He did for Israel, of a future that looks fruitful, prosperous, and full of joy—something we can look forward to, something we can hope for, which then activates our faith. It is usually something that looks impossible for us to receive or accomplish in our own strength.

Psalm 71:22 encourages us to believe God: "You are faithful to your promises, O my God" (NLT). Numbers 23:19 says, "God is not human, that he should lie, not a human being, that he should change his mind. Does he speak and then not act? Does he promise and not fulfill?" (NIV).

God's Word is filled with promises for His people. He knew that the human beings He had made would need assurances of His love and character in order to believe the promises He made to them. We need to know we can always count on God to do what He says He will do, that our trust in Him is not misplaced, and that He will never disappoint us.

When I go out of town on a ministry trip, my grandchildren often ask me to bring them back a present. When I look at their sweet faces, I cannot help but promise them that I will bring them something from my travels. And as soon as Tom and I arrive home, they run to me with great excitement, exclaiming, "What did you bring us?" (Their parents are normally exasperated, saying, "Say hi to Mimi and Papa first!") You see, I made a promise, and they have a childlike expectation that I will fulfill it.

So why do we have so much trouble believing that our heavenly Father will keep His promises to us?

I believe it is usually because there are obstacles to overcome in the midst of the process of seeing the promises fulfilled. For Abraham the obstacle to his faith was time. It took 25 years to see the promise of a son fulfilled. For Joseph it was betrayal. For Moses it was discouragement and people problems. For David it was the disdain of his own brothers and the problem of the old Saul order.

Everyone is given promises. And everyone faces challenges in seeing those promises fulfilled. The question is not whether God will fulfill His word to us. The question is whether we will remain faithful to Him in the midst of the trial until fulfillment comes.

Game-Players or Giant-Slayers?

Trials are designed to enhance our trust in the Lord. Each time we face an obstacle, it is our opportunity to see the goodness of God manifest in our lives in a new way. Hebrews 10:35–36 (ESV) exhorts us:

> Therefore do not throw away your confidence, which has a great reward. For you have need of endurance, so that when you have done the will of God you may receive what is promised.

Israel faced such a challenge. In Numbers 13 and 14 we see Israel on the brink of receiving her promise. God was excited to show her this awesome place He had prepared for her. He told Moses to choose one man from each tribe to go and spy out the land, to see the blessing He had in store for them. So Moses gathered the twelve spies, among them Joshua, the son of Nun, from the tribe of Ephraim, and Caleb from the tribe of Judah. *Ephraim* means "double fruit"[3] and *Judah* means "praise."[4] Perhaps these tribal characteristics helped these two men keep a proper, godly perspective as they went on their mission.

Moses gathered the twelve and gave them instructions for their journey:

> See what the land is like: whether the people who dwell in it are strong or weak, few or many; whether the land they dwell in is good or bad; whether the cities they inhabit are like camps or strongholds; whether the land is rich or poor; and whether there are forests there or not.
>
> Numbers 13:18–20

He did not tell them to do this to be afraid, but so that they could best strategize for taking the land. He added: "Be of good courage. And bring some of the fruit of the land" (verse 20). This was going to be an exciting trip!

On their journey they cut down some branches of big, juicy grapes. One cluster took two men to carry it. They also brought back pomegranates and figs. The produce in the land was amazing! It was everything God said it was—a land flowing with milk and honey.

But most of the spies said, "God forgot to mention the giants! The people of the land are strong. Their cities are huge and fortified. And there are tribes of giants there, men eight and nine feet tall. Do you remember the tribe of Amalekites we had to fight in the valley of Rephidim when we came out of Egypt? We barely beat them then, and now they're all over the south lands. Other tribes are there, too, all of them mightier than we are. We can't beat them. This land devours its inhabitants. The giants make us look like grasshoppers, little bugs they can just squash. There's no way we can win this. Why did God bring us out here to die? Our children will become victims of these giants. Let's choose new leaders and go back to Egypt."

Those ten spies were unwilling to rise to meet the challenge. All God's incredible promises were overshadowed by the perceived impossibilities. Rather than being the giant-slayers God had anointed them to be, they became game-players with the promises of God.

But two of the spies had a different story:

> Joshua son of Nun and Caleb son of Jephunneh, members of the scouting party, ripped their clothes and addressed the assembled People of Israel: "The land we walked through and scouted out is a very good land—very good indeed. If GOD is pleased with us, he will lead us into that land, a land that flows, as they say, with milk and honey. And he'll give it to us. Just don't rebel against GOD! And don't be afraid of those people. Why, we'll have them for lunch! They have no protection and GOD is on our side. Don't be afraid of them!"
>
> Numbers 14:6–9 MSG

Joshua and Caleb understood that if God was for them, who could be against them (see Romans 8:31)? They would eat giants for their bread. They had nothing to be afraid of. God was setting them up not for defeat and disappointment, but for victory.

These two men spoke the promise instead of the problem. As hard as it was to believe, the giants were there to be a blessing to Israel. Victory over them was part of God's redemptive plan for her people. He had proved Himself to them over and over, in delivering them from Egypt, in parting the Red Sea, in destroying Pharaoh's armies. Now He wanted them to experience the joy of being transformed from helpless slaves under Pharaoh to a mighty army that conquered giants. He wanted to use this victory to remove their old identity of bondage and prove to them that they were people of breakthrough. He wanted them to begin their new lives in the land of promise as victors, not victims. He wanted to turn their trials into triumphs. This would be the greatest breakthrough in the history of the world, and His people would be forever known as giant-killers.

Unfortunately, although God had been successful in getting Israel out of Egypt, it became clear that He had yet to succeed in getting Egypt out of them. All they could do was speak the problem; they could no longer see the promise.

Sadly, we know the story. The people could hear only the voices of fear and shame. They could no longer believe the promises of God. "We were like grasshoppers in our own sight, and so we were in their sight" (Numbers 13:33). So they remained slaves to their past. They rejected the amazing gift this extravagant God was offering them, and they were banished to wander in the wilderness for forty years until they all died out and a new generation arose. God would keep His promise, but it would be for another generation.

After Moses announced God's judgment to the people, they changed their minds and decided they wanted to cross over into the land after all. But they had missed their window of opportunity and were driven back by the Amalekites and Canaanites waiting on the other side, guarding the land of promise.

Confronting the Robber

Jesus' promise of abundant life in John 10:10 was preceded by His warning regarding the thief who comes to steal, kill, and destroy. The New Testament makes clear that this is the devil, whereas in the Old Testament a variety of enemies personified this thief.

The Amalekites were one of these warring tribes. They met Israel as they came out of Egypt (as we noted in the introduction), and were the first enemy Israel had to face as an army. They were fierce marauders and their reputation preceded them. First Samuel 14:48 calls them plunderers. They represented the spirit of robbery against God's people.

Tom and I had personal experience with this spirit. We were in a season of suffering, apparently at the hands of a spiritual robber. Financially we seemed to have a hole in our bucket and resources were draining out. Unexpected repairs and medical bills were challenging our budget. On several ministry trips, we were asked to send large quantities of books and CD sets overseas, as well as pay for our own airline tickets, all of which went unreimbursed, despite commitments to the contrary by those who had invited us. To top it off, I checked out of my hotel one morning and placed my suitcase in the vehicle of the people who would take me to the airport after the service. While I was preaching, someone stole that car. It was later recovered, but I never saw my jewelry or computer again.

During that time I asked the Lord what was happening, and He told me that an Amalekite spirit had been assigned against Tom and me to rob us of our peace, our prosperity, and our promise. As we prayed against this spirit, things started to turn around. Bills were paid miraculously. Supernatural supply came for our needs. God even convicted those who had refused to honor their commitment to reimburse us for our expenses, and they repaid us years later.

Throughout the centuries of biblical history, we see the Amalekites robbing the people of God—from the threshing floor of Gideon all the way to the attempted annihilation of the Jews during the time of Esther. How did this tribe rob the Israelites in the wilderness? They got them to abandon their faith and give place to fear. When it was time for the Israelites to possess the land, the Amalekites struck fear in the hearts of the people, so much so that they were willing to give up their destiny of possessing their land of promise. Even worse, the spirit of intimidation from this demonic stronghold convinced Israel that it would be better for her to return to a life of slavery in Egypt rather than rally to face this foe.

The Amalekites caused Israel to forget the promises of God. They got her to believe the lie that God was not able to do what He said. Denying God's power became a curse that the Israelites brought on themselves.

This tribe was bad news for God's people throughout history. But time and again God gave His people victory over them and brought recovery of all they had stolen.

It is easy for us to read the Scriptures today and picture Israel versus the giants. When we see her wanting to go back to Egypt, we may think, *Are you kidding me? Don't you remember what you have been delivered from?* Yet in our own lives, the enemy attempts to put us in the same position, forcing us to choose between the often uncomfortable challenge of facing our fears and advancing toward our destiny, or else retreating to a place that is comfortable for the flesh but unsatisfying for the spirit—a place God has not chosen for us.

Our own Amalekite enemy will try to threaten and intimidate us into submission by attacking our true identity. The Israelites should have remembered that God had declared them His chosen people. They were the people for whom God had worked miracles in Egypt. He opened the Red Sea for them so they could escape Pharaoh's armies, then watch as the sea closed over the chariots, destroying their enemies. He was the

God who healed the bitter waters at Marah and brought water out of a rock.

God had proved time and again that He was for them and not against them. Yet when faced with the relatively small issue of giants in the land, the Israelites wanted to turn around and run. Somehow they could never believe that God was a good God who loved them and desired to bless them. Israel had a wrong concept about God and a wrong understanding about her own identity.

Identity Theft

One of the first tactics the enemy uses to keep us from possessing our own prophetic promise is to commit identity theft and cause us to forget who we truly are in Christ. *Who do you think you are, anyway? What makes you think you deserve that blessing? Do you really think God has spoken to you? You think way too much of yourself.*

It is a tactic as old as the Garden of Eden, when the serpent said to Eve, "Did God really say you shouldn't eat that fruit? He is actually holding out on you. He knows that if you eat it, you will be like Him."

What is wrong with this statement? Eve was created in God's image and likeness. She was already like God. But the serpent stole her identity and she forgot who she was. In the process he took her destiny as well.

Once the enemy convinces you that God does not want to bless you, or that you are not good enough, smart enough, spiritual enough, old enough, young enough—or whatever lie he is using—it is easy for him to take your faith and your courage to completely disarm and discourage you. Before long you are embarrassed that you ever dreamed your prophetic promise could come true. Fear causes you to settle back into mediocrity—or, worse, intimidation and returning to an old lifestyle that was familiar and comfortable but full of bondage and defeat.

If, on the other hand, you discover and walk in your true identity in Christ, you will find the courage necessary to rise up and face your giants. Joshua and Caleb were unaffected by fear of the Amalekites because they were grounded in their identity as God's people: "God is on our side. Don't be afraid of these giants. Come on, people, take back your courage and fight to possess what God has given us."

The Robbers of Fear, Shame, and Pride

I hate fear. It is such a destiny robber! It robs us of hopes and dreams, and it has strangled faith out of some of the strongest believers. In fact, the enemy of fear was a stronghold in my own life.

I was never afraid of being in front of people. I was not afraid of failure or lack. But I had secret, hidden fears that were undermining my ability to be all God called me to be. I was afraid of the dark. I was terrified of snakes. And ultimately I was paralyzed by fear of the devil. All these were pretty embarrassing to me as a woman of faith and as a minister, so I fought my battles against them alone. I did not even tell my husband I was struggling. Why? Because of the shame I felt in admitting it.

Shame is an identity issue, and it was trapping me in my fear. And it partnered with pride, which kept me from reaching out for help. Shame stole my identity as an overcomer.

You see, a big part of my calling is to give people courage to face their own fears and inadequacies, and to rise up and be what God has called them to be. That is part of the prophetic nature and calling God created me for. Yet I was being conquered by the very fear I was called to defeat.

Fear, shame, and pride all worked together to keep me bound. For me to fulfill my prophetic calling, I needed to break out of all of those, repent, and be set free. Only then would I be free to bring the message of liberty to others. I had to humble myself and confess my faults to others, who could pray for me so that I could be healed (see James 5:16).

I did so. And not only did I receive freedom from fear, but now I have a passionate desire to see others set free from fear and the lies of shame and pride that the enemy brings.

Catching the Thief

I opened this chapter with the dream of my intercessor friend Brenda, in which she and her husband captured the robbers and asked, "Why are you robbing us?" One of the thieves answered, "Because I can." There was more to the dream, which will help us understand how we can take back our faith and courage and possess our prophetic promise. Here is the dream in Brenda's words:

> At the time of the dream, my husband and I were renting a house on stilts. Over the course of five years of marriage, every time we had saved up money to purchase a home, something unexpected would happen to steal our finances. Our bank account was accessed and drained, causing overdraft charges on all the checks we had previously sent out. We worked our way out of that debt. Then, for four consecutive years, the motors in our vehicles unexplainably blew up, different vehicles each time. One year in December, our work equipment was stolen from a storage area under our house. In January we found out that the home we were living in was being auctioned off in February, and we knew it was time to find and purchase our own home.
>
> But we didn't understand why we kept being robbed, so we asked the Lord why this was happening. We worked, tithed, served at the church, prayed, and *believed* to stop this constant robbing of our finances.

In February I had the dream. In the dream my husband and I were in the house, and we heard noises from below, in the storage area. We knew we were being robbed again and we ran downstairs to stop the thieves. I saw a shadow and said to my husband, "There he is!" My husband grabbed him, and I asked him, "Who are you and why do you keep stealing from us?" He said, "Because I can!" in an awful voice. I demanded that he tell me his name, or I would call the police. He looked at me with an evil grin and said, "My name is Shame."

As soon as he said it, I heard a noise behind us and turned to see another figure in hiding. I turned back to the man and asked, "Who is that?" He said, "That's my girlfriend. Her name is Pride."

At that point I woke up and told my husband that God had shown us what we had to deal with in prayer. The next morning we went to the courtroom of heaven and repented for ourselves and generations past for allowing shame and pride into our lives. Then we asked God to break any generational curses, loosing prosperity and generational blessings instead.

God declared us not guilty by the blood of Jesus and rendered a verdict on our behalf. We thanked and praised Him for showing us what the devil had against us, and for freeing us by what Jesus had done through His death and resurrection.

We believed it was over and that the spirit of robbery was gone, but God proved it two days later by bringing divine recovery. We were getting ready to go look for houses in our price range when we received a call from a woman who knew our situation. She said she knew we were looking at houses, and she wanted to give us $50,000 to get the house we wanted, not just the one we could afford.

From that day forward, we started receiving money and gifts totaling more than $64,000 for our new home. We experienced not just the breaking of a curse, but divine recovery of all the enemy had stolen.

I love how the Lord gives revelation, through His Word or dreams or visions, that enables us to break through barriers. Today Brenda and her husband have a beautiful house and are living in the blessings of the Lord. They were able to confront the thieves of shame and pride and gain victory to possess their promise.

Double for Your Trouble

Jesus came to set us free and redeem us from every type of curse and the shame that goes with it. Galatians 3:13 (NLT) says:

> Christ has rescued us from the curse pronounced by the law. When he was hung on the cross, he took upon himself the curse for our wrongdoing. For it is written in the Scriptures, "Cursed is everyone who is hung on a tree."

Jesus delivered us from the curse of sin and death. He set us free from every curse of sickness, poverty, and oppression. He conquered every enemy and has decreed a time of payback for our losses. Our generous, loving God did all it was possible to do, to demonstrate to us that He is for us, not against us. But we must appropriate the freedom Jesus died to give us, so we can receive the full recompense for what the devil owes.

Second Timothy 1:12 (TPT) says,

> The confidence of my calling enables me to overcome every difficulty without shame, for I have an intimate revelation of this God. And my faith in him convinces me that he is more than able to keep all that I've placed in his hands safe and secure until the fullness of his appearing.

Divine recovery does not mean just getting back what was stolen, but receiving double for your trouble. Exodus 22:7 tells us when we catch a thief, he must restore double. Proverbs 6:31 tells us when we catch a thief, he has to pay back seven times what he stole. After Zacchaeus, the tax collector, met Jesus, he said, "If I have taken anything from anyone by false accusation, I restore fourfold" (Luke 19:8). And Isaiah 61:7 declares:

> Instead of your shame you shall have double honor, and instead of confusion they shall rejoice in their portion. Therefore in their land they shall possess double; everlasting joy shall be theirs.

I love the way *The Message* says it:

> Because you got a double dose of trouble and more than your share of contempt, your inheritance in the land will be doubled and your joy go on forever.

Divine recovery means we can ask the Lord to cause the enemy to give back at least double of what he has stolen from us. That is a promise of double for our trouble.

A man in our church, Daniel Schaefer, acquired some equipment from a man who was found to be taking advantage of him continuously. Daniel made a list of his grievances and was preparing to contact the parent company to let them know. Instead God told him to bury the list in the bottom of his desk drawer and forgive him. Over time the man was going bankrupt and asked Daniel to make him an offer for his remaining equipment. Daniel did not have much money but offered what he could. The man was not happy, but ended up selling Daniel twice the value of what had been taken from him in previous deals. God brought him back double for his trouble.

A Prophetic Word for You

The Lord says: I am releasing a new mantle of courage on your life so you can rise up and confront the giants standing in your way. I am breaking off the spirits of fear, shame, and pride, as well as every limiting mindset. I am releasing great faith within you that will enable you to possess your prophetic promise. Don't look back to a previous season or familiar place, as Israel began to long for Egypt. Dare to look into the realm of the unknown, for it is there that your promised land awaits. Yes, there are giants there, but I have made you a giant-killer. Christ in you is the hope of glory. Through Me you can do all things. Now is the time to shake off the dust of defeat and disappointment and rise up to claim your promise. I will strengthen and empower you to accomplish all I have called you to, says the Lord your God.

Pray with Me

Lord, I repent of any lie I have believed about who You are or what Your intentions are toward me. I believe You are a good and loving Father, El Shaddai, the All-Sufficient One, and that You delight in meeting my needs. I repent of shame and pride, which have kept me in bondage, as well as the spirit of fear that has sought to control my life and crush my dreams. I ask that You restore double for my trouble and break the power of the spirit of robbery over my life. I eat giants for my bread! I will fulfill my destiny and possess my promised land. In Jesus' name. Amen.

QUESTIONS TO CONSIDER

1. What are some promises for your future that you feel God has given you?

2. What are some specific obstacles you are facing, preventing you from seeing His promises fulfilled?

3. What are some of the personal giants you face regularly?

THREE

TAKING BACK OUR PEACE

I have said these things to you, that in me you may have peace. In the world you will have tribulation. But take heart; I have overcome the world.

John 16:33 ESV

In prayer I heard the Lord say He wanted to tell me three things.

First, He told me to tell the people that chaos was going to increase in the earth. Well, I was not very excited about this word and did not think the people gathered at church that day would be, either. Chaos steals the peace from individuals, families, and even nations. Chaos causes anxiety and fear to take root in people's hearts.

But then I heard the Lord say, *Wait, there's more.*

Second, He said He was going to use chaos to strip the covering off corruption and expose things being done in secret that rob people, nations, and generations. The chaos coming would actually be useful in destroying hidden plans of the enemy and causing things done in darkness to come to light.

Third, I heard the Lord say, *Then tell them, "The God of peace is rising, the God of peace is rising, the God of peace is rising."* He specifically said that three times.

I knew this referred to Romans 16:20, which declares, "The God of peace will soon crush Satan under your feet" (NASB). The Greek word for peace is *eirene*, which means to join with prosperity, peace, quietness, rest, set at one again.[1] Thayer expands on this: "the state of national tranquility free from the rage and havoc of war, peace between individuals, harmony, safety, security, prosperity."[2]

There has been and continues to be a great deal of chaos in the nations of the earth. We are living in a time of great shaking, and God's people must know how to intercede in order for His will to be done in our lives and lands. Romans 16:20 has become a key verse to use in praying for nations. God desires to rise up as the God of peace to exercise authority in crushing Satan, who is called the one "who weakened the nations" (Isaiah 14:12).

As I pondered what the Lord was saying, I thought of Isaiah 9:6, which calls the coming Messiah the "Prince of Peace." The word for *prince* in Hebrew is *sar*, which means a head person, captain, or governor;[3] from the root word *sarar*, meaning to have dominion or to rule.[4] This is the picture of our Prince of Peace, Jesus Christ. He is not someone who wears a royal crown, sits on a throne, and waves to the crowd in a parade. No, our Prince of Peace is a warrior, a ruler. Everything is under His dominion. He is fighting for us! *Prince* is a warring word, yet it is paired with the word *peace*.

The Hebrew word for *peace* is *shalom*, often translated peace or rest. But *shalom* encompasses much more. It means to be safe, well, happy, friendly, healthy, prosperous, safe, and at rest.[5]

This word encompasses everything good in life. For this reason Jewish people often greet one another with the blessing *Shalom*.

God is rising as a warring, ruling Prince to crush Satan under His feet so we can experience all the good things life has to offer.

A few days after the Lord told me those three things in prayer, I was sharing them with one of my previous Bible college professors. He told me that he had been in a Bible study just that week with some Hebraic scholars who were teaching on the word *shalom*.

When rabbis look at a Hebrew word, he told me, they do not just take it at face value, but examine each letter used to spell the word. Hebrew is a pictorial alphabet, meaning there is a picture conveyed with the writing of each letter. The four letters used in Hebrew to write the word *shalom* are *shin*, *lamed*, *vav*, and *mem*. When the pictures associated with these letters are connected, the true, deeper meaning of the word *shalom* emerges, along the lines of "God's peace destroys the authority of chaos"; or "Peace comes when you destroy the authority of chaos."[6]

When we walk in God's peace, it releases a power that destroys the authority of chaos over our lives. When we pray, God rises as the God of peace and crushes Satan under His feet. God was telling me this was going to be a time of spiritual war, but the end result would be victory over chaos and the expansion of the Kingdom of God in the earth.

Contending for Peace

We noted earlier that the first time Israel had to assemble and fight as an army was against the spirit of robbery, the Amalekites. They did not go looking for a fight; the fight came to them. They had two choices: fight or die. Remember, the Amalekites always tried to steal the quality of life and the quantity of blessings from the people of God. They were a tribe of fierce warriors and Israel was a band of former slaves. But God wanted to show up in their midst as the God of peace to fight for them and through them to show them what was possible.

This first battle took place in the valley of Rephidim, which means "resting place."[7] To be clear, the enemy will try to steal your possessions, your finances, your marriage, your family, and your joy. But more than any of those things, the first thing the Amalekites came to rob was Israel's place of rest. If the enemy can keep you out of rest, he will steal your peace. If he can get you out of peace, you will operate in fear and doubt rather than faith. Then it becomes easy for the enemy to take everything else as well.

When we look at this first battle that Israel fought as an army, we find some valuable keys that enable us to operate in victory today when faced with peace-robbing circumstances. These keys also help us position ourselves to stand and see the God of peace rise on our behalf, supernaturally overthrow the enemy of chaos, and take back all he has stolen from us.

It may sound strange to say that we must fight for peace. The two words do not seem to go together. In Hebrews 4:11, however, God tells us to "labour . . . to enter into that rest" (KJV) or else, like Israel, we will fail.

Initially the Israelites did not enter the Promised Land because they never grasped the concept of entering into God's Sabbath rest or walking in the power of His peace. God was looking for them to trust Him, which would produce unlimited power. Time and again, however, they could look at the natural circumstances only with fear and anxiety rather than faith.

We learn from their shortcomings that we must be intentional in understanding the power of peace and how the enemy will do anything in his ability to rob us of this.

63

I preached on this subject at church one day. The following day I was put to the test. I was traveling for a ministry trip, but that morning my alarm did not go off. I had to rush around to get out the door but was determined not to lose my peace. I barely got to the airport in time to check my bag. I zipped through security and hurried to my gate. Then I saw that my flight was delayed. In fact, it was so late that I was going to miss my connections. But I reminded myself not to allow the enemy to steal my peace.

When I got seated on the plane, I found myself next to a very loud man who complained about everything. Rudely he pushed my arm off the shared armrest. Ugh! But I was determined not to lose my peace.

On my next flight, I was seated on the aisle, and while everyone was boarding, I got hit in the face with at least three backpacks. But I was not going to lose my peace. Finally a man was trying to maneuver a large carry-on in the overhead bin directly over my seat. You guessed it—he dropped it right on my head!

I have to admit, I lost my peace. I did not strike out at the man, but my head hurt, and I was frustrated the rest of that flight. But I had to make a decision to forgive the backpack-carriers and the suitcase-dropper and shake off my frustration. I prayed in the Holy Spirit (see Ephesians 6:18) and, by an act of my will, took my peace back.

I am not going to tell you it was easy. Usually it is not. But I knew that if the enemy stole my peace, I would not be able to be effective in the ministry of the Spirit once I got where I was going. I would be distracted and focused on challenging human circumstances rather than on the Kingdom of God. I had to fight to get back to a place of rest.

Jesus said, "My peace I give to you; not as the world gives" (John 14:27). Like many other spiritual blessings, such as salvation, healing, and freedom, peace has been provided for us—but we must choose to enter in and lay hold of it. That means we need to surrender our anxiety, fear, and stress to Him, regardless of the reality we are facing. God will enable us to enter the rest of faith, not struggling or striving for our salvation, but possessing the fullness of all Jesus has given.

Isaiah 26:3 says, "You will keep him in perfect peace, whose mind is stayed on You, because he trusts in You." I love how *The Passion Translation* says this: "Perfect, absolute peace surrounds those whose imaginations are consumed with you; they confidently trust in you." This is our prescription for peace.

Principles for Victory

Let's look at Israel's battle against the peace-robbing Amalekites to learn how we can position ourselves for victory:

> Now Amalek came and fought with Israel in Rephidim. And Moses said to Joshua, "Choose us some men and go out, fight with Amalek. Tomorrow I will stand on the top of the hill with the rod of God in my hand." So Joshua did as Moses said to him, and fought with Amalek. And Moses, Aaron, and Hur went up to the top of the hill. And so it was, when Moses held up his hand, that Israel prevailed; and when he let down his hand, Amalek prevailed. But Moses' hands became heavy; so they took a stone and put it under him, and he sat on it. And Aaron and Hur supported his hands, one on one side, and the other on the other side; and his hands were steady until the going down of the sun. So Joshua defeated Amalek and his people with the edge of the sword.
>
> Then the LORD said to Moses, "Write this for a memorial in the book and recount it in the hearing of Joshua, that I will utterly blot out the remembrance of Amalek from under heaven." And Moses built an altar and called its name,

The-LORD-Is-My-Banner; [Jehovah Nissi] for he said, "Because the LORD has sworn: the LORD will have war with Amalek from generation to generation."

Exodus 17:8–16

From this account we can identify six principles that will help us position ourselves for victory.

1. Establish a Connection with Heaven

At the time of battle, Moses went up to the mountaintop overlooking the valley of Rephidim and lifted the rod of God up to heaven. While he was on the mountain, Joshua and his troops were in the valley fighting with the sword. As long as Moses' hands were lifted, Israel prevailed. When he dropped his hands, Amalek prevailed. If Israel was going to win the battle over Rephidim, the "resting place," she would do so because heaven came to help her and because she had an established connection with God.

Moses' rod was a symbol of his connection with heaven, and his action in using the rod had a history of effectiveness. He had lifted it in Pharaoh's court back in Egypt, and demonstrated God's power by turning the rod into a serpent that swallowed up the serpents created by Pharaoh's magicians. He had lifted up the rod when he sent the ten plagues on the Egyptians, proclaiming on God's behalf, "Let My people go!" Moses lifted the rod at the Red Sea when faced with dire impossibility, and God turned disaster into a door for the supernatural, parting the Red Sea and allowing all Israel to walk across on dry ground.

We may not carry a rod with us in modern times, but each of us should have an effective, established history of connection to heaven. How do we connect with heaven? We connect through practicing the spiritual disciplines on a daily basis:

reading God's Word, memorizing Scripture, praying, worshiping, praying in the Holy Spirit, coming before His throne of grace to make decrees, and more. In short, we practice the presence of the Lord on a daily basis, and this positions us for victory.

The time of crisis is not the time to find out if your rod works. Moses walked with "the rod of God" for decades and proved its power time and again. James 5:16 tells us that "the earnest (heartfelt, continued) prayer of a righteous man makes tremendous power available [dynamic in its working]" (AMPC). We must develop a spiritual history of connecting with heaven, so that, when facing crisis, we may remind ourselves of all the times God has prevailed as a result of our prayers.

Moses connected to heaven with his arms upraised and the rod of God in his hand before Israel ever engaged in the battle. Moses acted as a conductor of heavenly power that opened the heavens and brought victory in the earth. This is also our job as intercessors and leaders. We must know how to stand—not just for ourselves, but as a heavenly conduit to release the Kingdom of heaven into the place of battle. It was for this reason that Jesus taught His disciples to pray, "Thy kingdom come. Thy will be done in earth, as it is in heaven" (Matthew 6:10 KJV).

2. Recognize the Battlefield Is the Mind

The battleground of your destiny begins in your mind! If you want to change your life, it has to begin by changing your mind. Your beliefs will inform your behavior. The enemy knows that if he can get you out of alignment with heaven and get the Word of God out of your mind, most of the battle is already won. He recognizes that we cannot defeat him in our own strength, so he will attack our minds and steal our peace. If he can convince you that "this is just life," he will keep you from even showing up to contend.

For this reason, Romans 12:2 (TPT) challenges us by saying:

Stop imitating the ideals and opinions of the culture around you, but be inwardly transformed by the Holy Spirit through a total reformation of how you think. This will empower you to discern God's will as you live a beautiful life, satisfying and perfect in his eyes.

In *The Three Battlegrounds*, Francis Frangipane writes:

You will remember the location where Jesus was crucified was called "Golgotha," which means "place of the skull." If we will be effective in spiritual warfare, the first field of conflict where we must learn warfare is the battleground of the mind; i.e., the "place of the skull." For the territory of the uncrucified thought-life is the beachhead of satanic assault in our lives. To defeat the devil, we must be crucified in the place of the skull. We must be renewed in the spirit of our minds.[8]

Joyce Meyer has written an entire book on the subject. In *Battlefield of the Mind*, she writes, "You cannot have a positive life and a negative mind."[9] We must understand how to combat the negative thoughts, doubts, fears, worries, anxieties, vain imaginations, and arguments that bombard our minds on a regular basis.

Remember that when Israel faced the Amalekites and the giants later, their response was not one filled with faith but fear. It had everything to do with their thought life. Recall Numbers 13:33: "We even saw giants there, the descendants of Anak. Next to them we felt like grasshoppers, and that's what they thought, too!" (NLT). For us to defeat the spirit of robbery, we need to get our stinking thinking into alignment with God's Word—otherwise the enemy will not only get into our heads but also get under our skin.

Paul's letter to the church at Philippi provides keys for winning this battle. Remember, Paul wrote this letter while he was imprisoned in Rome. Yet he wrote these powerful words of instruction for winning the battle in our minds:

> Be anxious for nothing, but in everything by prayer and supplication, with thanksgiving, let your requests be made known to God; and the peace of God, which surpasses all understanding, will guard your hearts and minds through Christ Jesus.
>
> Philippians 4:6–7

The word translated "guard" is the Greek word *phroureo*, which means to be a watcher in advance, to guard as a sentinel, to post spies at the gate;[10] or to protect by a military guard to prevent hostile invasion or keep the inhabitants of a besieged city from flight.[11] In other words, the peace of God acts as a military sentinel posted at the gate of the "heart" (our emotions, affections, passions, desires, feelings[12]) and the "mind" (perception, purpose, intellect, thought[13]) to prevent hostile invasion.

Paul goes on to instruct the Philippians how to win this victory:

> Finally, brethren, whatever things are true, whatever things are noble, whatever things are just, whatever things are pure, whatever things are lovely, whatever things are of good report, if there is any virtue and if there is anything praiseworthy— meditate on these things. The things which you learned and received and heard and saw in me, these do, and the God of peace will be with you.
>
> Philippians 4:8–9

When we meditate on good things, the God of peace rises up and fights for us.

3. Don't Fight Alone

When the Israelites were facing the Amalekites in the valley of Rephidim, the first thing Moses said to Joshua was, "Choose some people to go fight with you" (see Exodus 17:9). Moses knew the battle could not be won with his rod and Joshua's sword alone. It would take an army. It would also take intergenerational connection between Moses and Joshua to see the victory. Moses needed Joshua's sword, but Joshua needed Moses' rod. They needed each other.

So Moses went to the mountaintop and took Aaron and Hur with him. He was responsible to lift the rod up to God and pray. But even in that task, he did not go alone. As the battle raged, he grew weary and needed the other men to hold up his hands in the battle.

As believers we need to know who our Moses is, so we can hold up that person's arms in the battle. We also need to know our Aaron and Hur. Are you connected to people who can hold you up in the fight? The enemy's greatest strategy is to isolate and separate you and get you fighting all on your own.

Even prior to the COVID-19 lockdowns, scientists have studied the health benefits of social connection. A study from Brigham Young University found that those who have strong social connections with friends and family are fifty percent less likely to die early. Having low levels of social interaction is equivalent to being an alcoholic or smoking fifteen cigarettes a day. Social isolation is more harmful than not exercising and twice as harmful as obesity.[14]

Another study out of Duke University found a vast increase in social isolation among Americans. It made the staggering discovery that "25% of Americans have no meaningful social support at all—not a single person they can confide in," which is more than double the number from 24 years earlier.

The study also says more than fifty percent of all Americans have no close relationships outside of their immediate family. It identified social isolation as "a huge risk factor for the onset of major depression, which has more than doubled in prevalence" in the decade before the study. And it noted "growing evidence that isolation increases vulnerability to various forms of addiction."[15]

Remember, these studies were done prior to the 2020 lockdowns, so the statistics today are likely even worse. That means that in the United States, a nation of nearly 340 million people, some 85 million do not have a single person to confide in, and some 170 million have no close relationships outside their immediate family. This is especially strange in a country that claims to be at least 64 percent Christian.

No wonder the enemy is winning so many battles! We were created for connection. We should not fight our battles alone. It is not good for us spiritually, socially, mentally, emotionally, or physically. Like Moses, we need to choose some people who can fight with us.

4. Use Your Sword to Advance

In the battle over Rephidim, the resting place, Joshua had to actively swing his sword to defeat the enemy. Although Hebrews 4:11 instructs us to "labour . . . to enter into that rest" (KJV), we must understand that this is not a passive positioning, but one in which we actively engage in the spiritual battle, using the sword of the Spirit, the Word of God. In fact, right after we are told to labor, Hebrews 4:12 says:

> For the word of God is living and powerful, and sharper than any two-edged sword, piercing even to the division of soul and spirit, and of joints and marrow, and is a discerner of the thoughts and intents of the heart.

71

These two verses are connected. We must labor to enter rest, and we must use the sword of the Word of God to advance.

The Amplified Bible, Classic Edition expounds on Hebrews 4:11–12 in an enlightening way:

> Let us therefore be zealous and exert ourselves and strive diligently to enter that rest [of God, to know and experience it for ourselves], that no one may fall or perish by the same kind of unbelief and disobedience [into which those in the wilderness fell]. For the Word that God speaks is alive and full of power [making it active, operative, energizing, and effective]; it is sharper than any two-edged sword, penetrating to the dividing line of the breath of life (soul) and [the immortal] spirit, and of joints and marrow [of the deepest parts of our nature], exposing and sifting and analyzing and judging the very thoughts and purposes of the heart.

Our warfare with the Word of God to take back our rest must be intentional. We must be zealous, exert ourselves, and strive diligently to lay hold of our rest. We must be willing to fight the enemy using Scripture. We must also tune our spiritual ears to the voice of the Lord and listen for His word to us. Psalm 29:4 says, "The voice of the LORD is powerful." The word *powerful* in Hebrew, *koach*, means "force"—in other words, "The voice of the LORD is a force."[16] It breaks down walls. It causes us to triumph. It positions us to overcome. We wage war with the written Word of God and with our prophecies.

5. Press into Rest

When I was in my mid-twenties, Tom and I pioneered a prophetic church, and we were on the forefront of pioneering the prophetic movement, along with Tom's father, Bishop Bill Hamon, considered by many to be the father of the modern prophetic movement.

In addition to everything we were doing at the church, our ministry was conducting at least one conference every month, in which I was vitally involved. We also hosted a Friday Night School of the Holy Spirit, a venue for different prophetic ministers each week. Besides this, we had three small children under the age of three and a half, and my son was born with some challenges, so I was taking him to many medical appointments in another city. Those were crazy years. I was very busy.

During this time a prophet came to speak. He said, "Before I share from the Word, I have a prophetic word for Pastor Jane. The Lord says, 'You must labor to enter My rest. I am bringing you into a season of experiencing the peace of God. So rest, My daughter, rest.'"

Normally when I was involved with a church service, I was on the prayer team, the worship team, the dance team, and the prophetic team. But the next week, in an effort to obey the directive of this prophetic word, I was not on any of the teams. Rather than being up front, I spread a blanket on the floor for my kids, and was in the back of the sanctuary worshiping. I loved being involved, but I was working at entering into rest.

That week another prophet got up to speak. He said, "Before I begin, I have a word for Pastor Jane. Could you come up here, please?"

As I started walking up the aisle, he said, "The Lord says, 'What are you doing in the back of the church? This is not a season to rest but to press the battle to the full. Rise up, daughter, and press in to all I have for you.'"

I was pretty confused. So the next week I was back up front, not on teams but fully engaged. Again a new prophet was there, who said, "Before I preach tonight, I have a word for Pastor Jane."

The whole congregation started to laugh. This was three weeks in a row.

He said, "The Lord says, 'I am releasing peace over your life. Enter into My peace. Enter into My rest and I will bless you.'"

I went home from the service that night, put the kids to bed, and then went and sat before the Lord. I said, "Lord, one of us is confused! I am pretty sure it's me, but I really don't know what to think about these words. First You tell me to rest, then You tell me to press, then You tell me to rest again. I will do whatever You tell me, but I am confused about what You are asking of me."

I waited for a few minutes, then the Lord replied to me. He said, *Jane, the problem is, you don't understand rest. Rest is not about action; it's about attitude.*

As I processed what the Lord had said, I realized He was not asking me to stop doing any of the things I was doing. Instead He was telling me that I needed to get out of worry, fear, anxiety, and a performance mentality. I needed to stop letting vain imaginations run through my mind. I needed to anchor myself in His Word, rest in His promises, and stop stressing out about things I could not control. I had to fight to enter into that place of rest.

This powerful word from the Lord has served me all my years of ministry. He has helped me know I can be busy with all He has called me to in ministry, plus the relationship with my family, and still walk in rest rather than stress. When I start getting anxious or stressed out, I work at setting my mind on Him and His Word, and peace returns to my heart.

When we control our attitude and set our hearts on the Word of God, He rises up for us as the God of peace who crushes Satan under His feet. J. Sidlow Baxter said, "What is the difference between an obstacle and an opportunity? It is our attitude towards it. Every opportunity has a difficulty and every difficulty has an opportunity."[17]

When we engage in battle, we must fight forward. We cannot retreat, as Israel often did. We cannot begin something in the Spirit and then try to finish it in the flesh. We must continue to speak the Word of God and use it as a sword to advance and never retreat.

6. Build Altars of Remembrance

Finally, in the lessons we learn from Israel's first battle in the valley of Rephidim against the robbers, the Amalekites, we must celebrate the victories God gives.

In Exodus 17:14, after Aaron and Hur held up Moses' hands and Israel defeated the Amalekites, the Lord promised Moses "that I will utterly blot out the remembrance of Amalek from under heaven." So Moses built an altar of remembrance and called it Jehovah-Nissi, "The-LORD-Is-My-Banner" (verse 15).

Why were they instructed to build altars? Because God wanted them to remember the victories He had brought. He is Jehovah-Nissi, "The LORD is my banner," and His victory standard flies over the camp of Israel. You see, God knew that not too long in their future, they would face these same enemies. He wanted it emblazoned on their minds that the same God who gave them victory that day would once again cause them to triumph.

Remembering past victories gives an opportunity to testify of God's goodness. God told Moses to write down this victory and rehearse it in the ears of Joshua (see Exodus 17:14). Telling the stories of triumph inspires and gives courage to future generations. As a matter of fact, the word *testimony* in Hebrew comes from a root word that means to duplicate or repeat;[18] to restore or redo it.[19] When we speak of what God has done, it opens the heavens for Him to come down and do it again. This builds faith and releases peace in our hearts regarding God's intentions of victory for us.

Second Thessalonians 3:16 (TPT) declares:

> Now, may the Lord himself, the Lord of peace, pour into you his peace in every circumstance and in every possible way. The Lord's tangible presence be with you all.

A Prophetic Word for You

The Lord says: *I am Jehovah Shalom, your peace. I never get stressed or worried or fearful. I am Peace personified. I have created you in My image and likeness, and, therefore, you can manifest My peace in every circumstance you face. I am your peace. When the enemy seeks to steal your peace, run to Me, and then reach out to others to maintain peace in your heart and mind. I am the God of peace and will crush Satan under your feet. Let My overwhelming love give you confidence that I will always fight for you, will never leave you, and will fill your very being with peace. I will reverse the years of stress and striving and will replace them with rest and thriving. This is your portion in Me, says the Lord your God.*

A Decree to Take Back Your Peace

[Speak this aloud in faith!] *I decree that the God of peace is rising on my behalf to crush Satan under His feet. Peace is my weapon to fight the enemy. I have authority over chaos. The peace of God rules my life and guards my heart and mind. My emotions, my thoughts, my intellect, my passions, my desires, and my feelings will all bow to the Lordship of Jesus Christ. I do not fight alone, but will stand with my leaders and be fortified by friends and family who stand with me. I will fight with the Word of God as my sword and will wage war with every prophetic promise God has given me. Today I take back my peace in every circumstance and in every possible way, and I declare divine recovery of all that has been stolen from me, by the authority of the name of Jesus Christ and the power of His Word.*

QUESTIONS TO CONSIDER

1. What are some things that are trying to rob your peace?
2. Can you identify any toxic thought processes that need to change?
3. Make a list of positive things you can focus on when under attack.
4. Who is your Moses whom you uphold and support?
5. Who are some of your Aarons and Hurs whom you can count on being in the fight with you?

FOUR

Taking Back Our Prosperity

As for every man to whom God has given riches and wealth, and given him power to eat of it, to receive his heritage and rejoice in his labor—this is the gift of God.

Ecclesiastes 5:19

A re you a dreamer? Do you imagine doing big things for God? Do you believe you are called to do more than what seems ordinary? I love a quote I once heard: "People of vision see the invisible, hear the inaudible, believe the incredible, think the unthinkable, and do the impossible." We will often *not* do the impossible things unless we can dream of the invisible things. Proverbs 29:18 encourages us that "where there is no vision, the people perish" (KJV).

God loves dreamers! Dreamers have big vision and often need big resources to accomplish that vision. This involves a faith journey of unlocking financial supply to accomplish all that God has put into their hearts. If you have limited expectations regarding resources, it will ultimately affect the expanse of your dreams. Limited expectations result in limited vision.

When Tom and I set out to build a ministry in Florida, we had big dreams for building a training center and a local church, making an impact locally but also reaching the world. Unfortunately we had very little money in our bank account to accomplish this dream. I could write an entire book about the times God was faithful to come through for us, often at the last moment, to meet our needs and fund advancement.

Through these years I personally had to confront a poverty mindset that placed limitations on our personal prosperity, and also on our ability to move forward with all God had spoken to us. I recognized that poverty and prosperity were opposite states of mind and could not function in the same space. So I had to develop a biblical understanding of what prosperity is, in order to see breakthrough happen, not just for our family but for our church, ministry, and territory as well. I had to realize it was not all about money, but it was also about not being afraid of the blessings and abundant provision of the Lord.

What a shock to realize that I had been an accomplice in my own robbery! My mindsets of poverty and unbelief were actually opening a door for the enemy to keep our family in constant lack. As I studied the Scriptures on the subject, I realized I needed to renew my mind and repent of unbiblical perspectives on wealth, finances, and prosperity, so God could take the limits off and I could dream bigger and believe my dreams could come true.

The Beginning of Prosperity

The word *prosperity* means "a successful, flourishing, or thriving condition, especially in financial respects."[1] In Hebrew it is the word *tsalach*, which means to push forward, to break out, to be profitable, to cause to prosper,[2] or simply to advance.[3] In Greek it is the word *euodoo*, which means to help on the road, to succeed in business affairs, to succeed in reaching, to have a prosperous journey.[4]

In short, prosperity is about financial blessings and success—but it is about much more. Third John 1:2 says, "Beloved friend, I pray that you are prospering in every way and that you continually enjoy good health, just as your soul is prospering" (TPT).

So when the thief comes to attack, he will attempt to deprive you of the fruit of your labor. He will try to steal your joy and peace and cut off your supply lines. He will stand in the way of your blessings and your success. He will try to take your money. It is time to identify the robber and what has been stolen and begin to take it back.

Sometimes robbery can be seen in an investment that goes bad or an economic downturn. At other times it can be a mounting up of small issues that drain savings, health, and energy. It can be something as drastic as lost contracts or getting laid off from a job or an actual physical robbery. It can be an unexpected illness that brings a mountain of medical bills.

The temptation in these situations is to adopt the "this is just life" mentality rather than requiring the enemy to pay you back.

In Judges 6 we see the old enemy, the Amalekites, robbing the people of God. This time they are teamed up with the Midianites, whose name means brawling or contention.[5] Strife will steal mental and emotional well-being, and also cause division and destruction along the way. The situation with Israel was actually a judgment from the Lord, as she had fallen into her patterns of idolatry once again. God had allowed these enemies to rob Israel, not to strike her with His anger, but that she might repent and turn back to Him—which is often a pattern of God dealing with His people.

Picture God's generous hand of blessing upon Israel. He fights for her, protects her, and provides for her. His delight is to do her good and to shelter her from every foe. But when the Israelites worshiped other gods, they were, in essence, saying, "We don't need You, Jehovah. We will worship who we want, when we want, and how we want." When that occurred, God merely lifted His hand of goodness from them for a short time, causing them once again to recognize that all their blessings and protection actually did proceed from the Lord, and repent. This is true revival and the beginning of prosperity.

Let this be a warning to us individually, and also to nations that have signaled their independence from the hand of the Lord. Oh, we say we want His blessings, but we don't want His requirements or His interference in our lives or in our lands. We say, "We've got this, God. We don't need to put our trust in You. We will live how we want, and worship if, when, and whomever we choose." When we respond to God's goodness and blessing in such a way, we should not be surprised when we experience a struggling economy, hardship, strife, and division in our nations. We should be crying out in repentance for our wayward hearts, standing in the gap for our land, and declaring our dependence on God. We must cry out for revival!

What is amazing is that God always forgives His people and then proceeds to punish those He uses to bring them back. Not only that, but God assures His people that there is recovery of everything that was taken from them in the process. True prosperity, we see, comes by turning our hearts back to God.

Many testify of having plenty of money but also having a broken heart, a difficult marriage, or a dysfunctional family. First Timothy 6:10 tells us, "The love of money is the root of all evil" (KJV). Money is not the root, but the love of money is. Prosperity must be put into proper perspective to be a true blessing.

Contending for Our Harvest

In Judges 6 we read the story of God turning the Israelites back to Himself and delivering them from their robbers. The enemies robbed them of their provision as well as their dignity. They either destroyed all the increase of the land or fed it to their own cattle. They stripped Israel of everything that was theirs and caused them to live low, humiliated, and broken.

> The children of Israel did evil in the sight of the LORD. So the LORD delivered them into the hand of Midian for seven years, and the hand of Midian prevailed against Israel. Because of the Midianites, the children of Israel made for themselves the dens, the caves, and the strongholds which are in the mountains. So it was, whenever Israel had sown, Midianites would come up; also Amalekites and the people of the East would come up against them. Then they would encamp against them and destroy the produce of the earth as far as Gaza, and leave no sustenance for Israel, neither sheep nor ox nor donkey. For they would come up with their livestock and their tents, coming in as numerous as locusts [the KJV says *grasshoppers*]; both they and their camels were without number; and they would enter the land to destroy it. So Israel was greatly impoverished because of the Midianites, and the children of Israel cried out to the LORD.
>
> Judges 6:1–6

Because of their sin, Israel was "greatly impoverished." This meant more than that they lacked supply. The word *impoverished* means they were feeble, oppressed, brought low, dried up, emptied, made thin.[6] They were languishing rather than flourishing as God intended. Their spirits were broken, and once again they saw their enemy as profoundly stronger, and they themselves vastly outnumbered. It was as if the words of a previous generation of Israelites echoed once again: "We were like grasshoppers in our own sight, and so we were in their sight" (Numbers 13:33).

As a result, the Israelites lived as fugitives in dens and caves. That was no way to thrive, to raise a family, to establish a home with crops and flocks. This was not the land of promise God had given them. Once again they focused on the problem—the oppression of their enemies—instead of on God's promise. They needed revival.

But God always has a plan for redemption and revival to remind His people of who He is and who they are. He begins by sending a prophet.

Call to Repentance

Prophets are the voice of God in the earth. Part of their job is to declare God's purposes and promises. Another part is to speak words that penetrate the hardest hearts so that men and women can turn to the Lord.

> And it came to pass, when the children of Israel cried out to the LORD because of the Midianites, that the LORD sent a prophet to the children of Israel, who said to them, "Thus says the LORD God of Israel: 'I brought you up from Egypt and brought you out of the house of bondage; and I delivered you out of the hand of the Egyptians and out of the hand of all who oppressed you, and drove them out before you and gave you their land. Also I said to you, "I am the LORD your God; do not fear the gods of the Amorites, in whose land you dwell." But you have not obeyed My voice.'"
>
> Judges 6:7–10

God is still sending prophets today to reveal human hearts. When people hear something from a prophet that he or she has no way of knowing in the natural realm, it makes Jesus real. When Jesus is made real, they must confront the message of the Gospel, which involves repenting and turning their hearts to Him.

I was ministering prophetically at Mercy Multiplied, a work founded by my dear friend Nancy Alcorn. It is a place where young women go to get free of life-controlling issues through the power of God's Word, amazing counselors, and the Holy Spirit. Thousands of women have had their lives transformed at these homes. Each year I go in with a team and minister prophetically to each resident in each home.

In the beginning they were terrified of what God might say to them, since most had lived broken, trouble-filled lives. But God speaks His plans and purposes over these women and woos them by His great love. It is a beautiful experience. As a prophet, I am not there to shame them or reveal their sin, but to demonstrate to each one how real God is, and in doing so lead them back to Him.

Even so, that does not mean God will not challenge these young women directly regarding issues in their lives.

On one occasion a young woman with an angry demeanor kept staring me down as I taught and prophesied over the other residents. She would roll her eyes as if to say, "This is a bunch of nonsense. I'm not having any part of it." At one point she got up, stomped out of the room, and slammed the bathroom door. I heard the Lord say, *As soon as she returns, I want you to minister to her.*

As she came back into the room and plopped down in her chair, I said, "Could I just go ahead and minister to you now?"

She replied, "Whatever," with an additional eyeroll.

Before I tell you what the Lord said to her, allow me to tell you what she later said she did when she stomped out and went into the bathroom. She walked back and forth and said to God, "I don't believe any of this stuff is real. As a matter of fact, I don't even think You are real. All my life I have asked You question after question, and You have never once answered me. If You are real, You'd better prove it to me today." Then she came back and plopped down with an exasperated sigh.

That is when I asked if I could minister to her.

Let me show you the goodness of God. She was clearly not in a good place spiritually. She was angry. She was broken. She seemed to have no faith in God. But when I laid my hands on her and began to prophesy, this is what the Lord said: "My daughter, I believe in you, even though you say you don't believe in Me. You say all your life you have asked Me question after question, and I have never answered you. Because I am God, I don't have to prove Myself to you. But because I love you, I *will* prove Myself to you."

Honestly, I did not understand much of the rest of the prophecy, because God was holding a one-way conversation with this young woman, answering her questions. She began to weep.

And when I got done, she got up, grabbed the microphone, and said to the group, "You guys! I just found out God is real!" She proceeded to tell them what she had said to God and how the prophetic word answered her cry and her questions directly.

So I asked her, "Are you ready to give your life to Jesus and receive Him as your Savior now?"

She said, "Absolutely!"

God still sends prophets today to call us back to Him. This is the picture of divine recovery: A life that was lost is now found and serving God wholeheartedly.

Call to Attention

After the Lord sent a prophet to the children of Israel, He sent an angel:

The Angel of the LORD came and sat under the terebinth tree which was in Ophrah, which belonged to Joash the Abiezrite, while his son Gideon threshed wheat in the winepress, in order to hide it from the Midianites. And the Angel of the LORD appeared to him, and said to him, "The LORD is with you, you mighty man of valor!"

Gideon said to Him, "O my lord, if the LORD is with us, why then has all this happened to us? And where are all His miracles which our fathers told us about, saying, 'Did not the LORD bring us up from Egypt?' But now the LORD has forsaken us and delivered us into the hands of the Midianites."

Judges 6:11–13

This angel was sent to get Gideon's attention. God wanted to reveal to him that, as he was hiding out and threshing wheat in a winepress, afraid of his enemies, God saw him as a "mighty man of valor."

This "Angel of the LORD" may not have been an ordinary angel. Many believe this to be a manifestation of the pre-incarnate Christ. Whether this was a messenger angel or Christ Himself, Gideon was to heed the divine words.

Gideon's first response was to accuse God of forsaking the Israelites, when actually the Israelites were the ones who had rejected the Lord.

Often individuals resist the call of God for the same reason. They blame and accuse and distrust God, when in truth He is blameless. Often it is their own hearts that have led them astray in the midst of conflict with the enemy. At times God will send a friend, a prophet, even an angel to draw them back to Himself.

Angels are seen interacting with people in the Bible from Genesis through Revelation, often bringing messages from the throne of God. Hebrews 1:14 tells us that angels are sent to assist "those who will inherit salvation." They are around us constantly, yet they operate in the unseen, supernatural realm. Only on occasion does God allow them to show themselves to humans in the natural realm. Angels protect, position, and provide for us, whether we see them or not.

When an angel shows up, it will get your attention. He does not come to chat; he carries an important message. He is on business for the King. He is not to be worshiped. He is not there to become your friend. He is an emissary sent to get you into position, so you can accomplish God's purpose in the earth. Angels are sent to help us recover all the enemy has stolen.

Call to Connection

First God sent a prophet to Israel; then He sent an angel (who was quite possibly the pre-incarnate Christ). The language in the verse changes from "The Angel of the LORD said . . ." to "The LORD said . . ." It was clear: God wanted a relationship with Gideon. He wanted to connect with him. He knew it would take this type of interpersonal communication to convince Gideon of who he was called to be and what his assignment was.

> Then the LORD turned to him and said, "Go in this might of yours, and you shall save Israel from the hand of the Midianites. Have I not sent you?"
>
> So he said to Him, "O my Lord, how can I save Israel? Indeed my clan is the weakest in Manasseh, and I am the least in my father's house."
>
> And the LORD said to him, "Surely I will be with you, and you shall defeat the Midianites as one man."
>
> Judges 6:14–16

The Creator of the universe showed up to talk with Gideon, but he was so steeped in failure and defeat that he could not fathom what God was saying to him. He argued with God. (I am sure no one reading this book has ever argued with God!) But the Lord continued to be patient with Gideon. Thank God He is patient with us as well.

God was preparing Gideon for an epic mission against the robbers and plunderers—destroyers, really—and God knew Gideon would need every bit of faith in Him to accomplish it.

For this reason God often sends signs and confirmations to strengthen our faith as well.

A Call to Courage

Israel needed to turn back to the Lord, and she needed a champion to lead and inspire her. After the Lord sent fire down onto the sacrifice Gideon offered, he rose to answer the call, which was a revelation of who God is and who he was called to be:

> Now Gideon perceived that He was the Angel of the LORD. So Gideon said, "Alas, O Lord GOD! For I have seen the Angel of the LORD face to face."
>
> Then the LORD said to him, "Peace be with you; do not fear, you shall not die." So Gideon built an altar there to the LORD, and called it The-LORD-Is-Peace.
>
> Judges 6:22–24

It is interesting that Gideon named the altar The-LORD-Is-Peace, Jehovah Shalom, especially when we recall the deeper meaning of *shalom*. Gideon was not just extolling the God of peace and prosperity, but the God who was rising up to take authority over the chaos that had ruled the land. Gideon was proclaiming God as the One who would fight for Israel to defeat the plunderers. He was rising up to bring divine recovery of all the enemy had stolen from them as a people and as a nation.

God is always looking for champions—those willing to stand up and make a difference in a land.

Champions must also be willing and able to face their fears. I used to think the definition of courage is the absence of fear. But I later learned it is actually "the ability to control your fear in a difficult or dangerous situation."[7] I used to think God could not use me to do great things because I had so many areas of fear in my life. But when I realized I could still be courageous, a champion, if only I would subdue fear, I felt empowered to do and be what God had called me to do and be, even if it meant facing danger. I will talk more about how I learned this in chapter 7.

Curses That Steal Your Blessing

The Amalekites represent not only a spirit of robbery, but many of the ways the enemy seeks to entrap us in a curse, keeping us out of God's blessings. God's heart has always been to turn the curse into a blessing (see Deuteronomy 23:5) if only we would love and serve Him. These curses become powerless when confronted with a repentant heart and the power of the blood of Jesus.

Here are three of the ways the enemy seeks to ensnare us.

Generational Curses

The Amalekites were descendants of Esau, Jacob's older brother. If you recall, God said He loved Jacob but hated Esau (see Romans 9:13). Esau represents following the flesh, while Jacob, as flawed as he was, represents pursuing one's spiritual inheritance. Jacob valued the blessing given to his grandfather, Abraham, and his father, Isaac, while Esau despised his birthright—which Jacob stole.

All Esau's descendants throughout Israel's history are seen making war with Israel. Esau's descendants represent generational curses, which constantly attempt to steal abundant life and blessings. But God reveals His nature as both loving and just, righteous yet compassionate:

> The LORD, the LORD God, merciful and gracious, longsuffering, and abounding in goodness and truth, keeping mercy for thousands, forgiving iniquity and transgression and sin, by no means clearing the guilty, visiting the iniquity of the fathers upon the children and the children's children to the third and the fourth generation.
>
> Exodus 34:6–7

God's first choice is always to confer generational blessings. At times we see curses and consequences of sin and iniquity following family lines. Some of this is because spiritual strongholds love to infect family lines. For this reason we may see a long line of alcoholics in one family, or a lineage of certain sicknesses causing premature death. Some of these can be attributed to behaviors that are taught generationally. But they can also become a pathway for demonic spirits to follow, luring family members into destructive behaviors that trap them in the same patterns as previous generations.

I ministered to a sweet young woman who was battling all kinds of addictions—alcohol, drugs, and sex—and self-destructive patterns in her life. As I prayed, I discerned a generational pattern of sexual abuse, rape, and violence. As I spoke with her about this, she shared that every woman in her family back to her great-grandmother had been the victim of child rape, abusive relationships, or pregnancy out of wedlock. These women suffered from the same addictive patterns she had. When I prayed with her, she repented of sinful behaviors, bad decisions, and ungodly beliefs regarding her life.

Once generational patterns were broken, the demonic spirit of abuse lost access to her and she was set free. For the first time in her life, she experienced joy instead of sadness. And she went on to experience complete life transformation through Christ. She got married and is the mother of many children, who are all serving the Lord.

The power of the blood of Jesus broke a generational curse and set her free to discover the life she was created to live.

How would a generational curse affect issues of poverty and prosperity? It could be through demonic spirits that have developed a stronghold attached to bloodlines in which sin regarding finances has occurred. Greed, avarice, slavery, robbery, injustice, extortion, and more—all can open a door to evil spirits that can affect generations. A generational curse could also be inflicted through mindsets and wrong attitudes toward money, exhibited and passed from one generation to the next. I once spoke to someone who said, "My parents were poor, my grandparents were poor, and I will always be poor." This fatalistic thinking holds people in bondage.

Within Christian circles, wrong mindsets might be established by intentional or subconscious vows of poverty, in which wrong biblical theology promotes the idea that to be poor is to be spiritual. This can often be seen in people with roots in Catholic or Pentecostal spiritual teaching. On the other side, some teachers promote the idea that to be rich indicates being spiritual. Neither extreme is true.

These are examples of mindsets or theologies that open the door generationally to the robber. Generational curses are broken when we repent of and renounce our agreement with those ways of thinking, and command every demonic spirit that may have come through family lines to cease and desist in their activities of limitation, lack, and poverty. The power

91

of the blood of Jesus breaks every curse and grafts us into His bloodline, giving us access to all of heaven's blessings.

Territorial Curses

Can a land be cursed? Can people living in a land come under the oppression of demonic spirits occupying that space? The Amalekites were called "valley dwellers," but they occupied certain desert places that were under their control. The conflict came whenever God's people crossed into their territory.

First we must understand that no part of this earth belongs to Satan or his demonic forces. Psalm 24:1 declares, "The earth is the LORD's, and the fulness thereof; the world, and they that dwell therein" (KJV). Lands and territories do not belong to the devil, regardless of how many occult or idolatrous practices are performed there.

Paul describes Satan as "the god of this world" (see 2 Corinthians 4:4 KJV), which can also be translated "the god of this present age."[8] When Satan offered Jesus the kingdoms of this world, he was offering to give Him rulership over the illegitimate kingdoms and systems operating in the earth realm. The earth itself was never his to give. Psalm 115:16 declares, "The heaven, even the heavens, are the LORD's; but the earth He has given to the children of men." The devil is a usurper, however, and attempts to lay claim to that which is not his. For this reason, Satan tries to control actual lands and territories, as well as the kingdoms of the world operating within them. This is why we need to dispossess him.

For example, Ephesus was the center of the ancient world for magic and occult training, as well as for the goddess worship of Artemis. Yet it did not belong to Satan. Revival broke out in Ephesus, and people burned their magic books worth tens of thousands or even millions of dollars. It became a base for Christianity to reach the ancient world.

The devil always tries to exercise illegitimate control over things that do not belong to him. The problem comes when God's people show up in the same space. Someone is going to rule.

This happened with Tom and me forty years ago when we moved to the beautiful Florida panhandle. We were not here long before we realized that this pristine beach town was actually full of occult groups. Satanists, witches, psychic healers, psychic gurus, pagans, spiritualists, and Santeria voodoo cults were among the groups we identified as operating in our land. Some of these cult members threatened us and our ministry staff members by spilling blood on our property, writing curses on our buildings, and even leaving decapitated animals on the doorsteps of our homes. From time to time we would discover sacrificial altars with our names and pictures on them.

As disconcerting as this was, we realized that Jesus had given us authority not only to pray for the people of our community, but literally to possess the land. We walked and prayed, took Communion in different locations, fasted, decreed, and did prophetic acts, until we saw those occult groups move out of our area one by one. Unlike Israel, we were not going to allow the Amalekites to keep us from settling in the land God had called us to.

But even when, one by one, those occult groups moved out, we found that the land was still locked up by a spirit of poverty. Of the 67 counties in Florida, we were ranked 64th on the economic scale. We had to pray and break territorial demonic assignments off our area. (I talk about strategies that bring transformation in my book *Discernment: The Essential Guide to Hearing the Voice of God.*) Today our county is one of the most prosperous in Florida. We have some of the best schools, law enforcement, and business communities in the state. Through prayer, we broke spiritual strongholds and have seen incredible change, all to the glory of God.

Self-Participating Curses

These are curses that come because we form an agreement with the wrong things and, as a result, enter into sin.

When Balak hired Balaam to curse the people of God, Balaam said he could not curse them because "the shout of a King is among them" (Numbers 23:21) and he knew they were God's people. But since he could not pronounce a curse over those God had blessed, he tried another strategy to win the favor and money of Balak: He told him that if he could trick Israel into sin, the door would be open for the curse to come. Their own sin caused a curse upon their lives. (See Numbers 31:16 and Revelation 2:14.)

Concerning the spirit of robbery, Malachi 3:8–9 says:

> Will a man rob God? Yet you have robbed Me! But you say, "In what way have we robbed You?" In tithes and offerings. You are cursed with a curse, for you have robbed Me, even this whole nation.

If someone is not walking in financial covenant with God, the devourer will claim he has access to their lives. I can pray for that person, prophesy over him or her, cast out demons, and make decrees, but it's not going to bring that person financial breakthrough. The solution is obedience. God says:

> "Bring all the tithes into the storehouse, that there may be food in My house, and try Me now in this," says the LORD of hosts, "if I will not open for you the windows of heaven and pour out for you such blessing that there will not be room enough to receive it. And I will rebuke the devourer for your sakes, so that he will not destroy the fruit of your ground, nor shall the vine fail to bear fruit for you in the field," says the LORD of hosts; "and all nations will call you blessed, for you will be a delightful land," says the LORD of hosts.
>
> Malachi 3:10–12

When I was first born again, I went to a Baptist church that taught me the basic disciplines of the Christian walk: reading my Bible, praying, attending church, and giving a tithe, or ten percent, of what I earned to the Lord. They explained that everything I had belonged to Him—one hundred percent—but that He asked for only ten percent back. If I gave Him my ten percent, the other ninety percent would be blessed; but if I kept the ten percent, one hundred percent of my money would be susceptible to the devil. (I don't think they wanted to use the word *cursed*, but that was what they were describing.) Since then I have always prioritized giving my tithe; and later I learned about the blessing of giving offerings. My needs have always been met.

Most Christians have probably heard the Malachi passage quoted at church, perhaps during the taking of the offering. Tom and I have served as senior leaders of a local congregation for almost forty years now, and we have used this passage as instruction to believers to give out of a positioning of covenant with God. Essentially if we keep the ten percent, we are taking what belongs to God and using it for our own needs or desires—and setting ourselves up for the robber.

I was witnessing to a man once who said he had stopped going to church because he got tired of their asking for his money. I understand that this can make people uncomfortable. As leaders, however, we teach this for the sake of the individual and his or her family. We teach it not because churches need their money, but because we understand the blessings that come through obedience in following scriptural principles. When we tithe, the devourer is rebuked and the windows of heaven are opened. Who does not want that?

Romans 2:22 addresses this subject: "You who say, 'Do not commit adultery,' do you commit adultery? You who abhor idols, do you rob temples?" In the King James translation, that last phrase reads, "Dost thou commit sacrilege?" You may ask what that has to do with this discussion. It is found in the word *sacrilege*, which in the Greek means to be a temple robber or robber of churches[9]—in other words, a God robber. *The Passion Translation* makes it a bit clearer:

> You are swift to tell others, "Don't commit adultery!" but are you guilty of adultery? You say, "I hate idolatry and false gods!" but do you withhold from the true God what is due him?

God is a generous, loving God. All He asks for is the ten percent that belongs to Him as a sign of our covenant with Him. Abraham tithed to Melchizedek long before the Law was ever given. Jesus spoke of tithing when He referred to the practices of the Pharisees:

> But woe to you Pharisees! For you tithe mint and rue and all manner of herbs, and pass by justice and the love of God. These you ought to have done, without leaving the others undone.
>
> Luke 11:42

There are other mindsets, ungodly beliefs, and unbiblical practices that can prevent the blessings of the Lord from flowing freely and can open the door to the enemy in our lives. I will discuss these in the next chapter. The key is to see what Scripture says, to repent of any area in our lives that is out of alignment, and then to watch how God proves Himself over and over again.

Taking Back Prosperity

The enemy loves nothing more than to trap, trick, or try the faith of believers, especially in the area of finances. The Amalekites and Midianites of old were the plunderers of the land, killing the dreams of an entire generation of Israelites.

But just as God raised up Gideon to partner with Him then, He is raising up men and women and young people today who know their God, who know their enemy, and who know themselves, and who are willing to do whatever is needed to take back what the enemy has stolen.

It is a spiritual battle, but the spoils of war just may be God's provision to fund the vision He has given you to fulfill. What are you waiting for?

A PROPHETIC WORD FOR YOU

The Lord says: *I stand ready to meet your needs according to My riches in glory by Christ Jesus. I never lack. I never fail. I own the cattle on a thousand hills. I long to give you the keys to your breakthrough and advancement. Turn to Me with all your heart. Seek first My Kingdom and My righteousness and I will add all these things unto you. As you keep covenant with Me with your tithes and offerings, I am ready to open the windows of heaven over your life and pour out abundant blessings on you and your family. I will rebuke the devourer for your sake and will decree blessing over your land. I will show you how to prosper and will withhold no good thing from you because of My great love for you. Put your trust in Me and see what I will do, says your God.*

A DECREE TO TAKE BACK YOUR PROSPERITY

[Speak this aloud in faith!] *I am blessed and not cursed. God loves me and desires to fill my life with His goodness in every*

97

area. He will provide for the vision He has given me and will supply my every need. In Jesus' mighty name.

QUESTIONS TO CONSIDER

1. What is your dream? How much money will it take to see your dream fulfilled?
2. Can you identify any area of prosperity that has been stolen from you?
3. Is there any area of your life that needs to be turned back to God?
4. Pray and ask the Holy Spirit to help you identify any areas of generational curses or mindsets that need to be repented of and broken off.
5. Can you identify any unbiblical belief you may have regarding God's blessing and prosperity in your life? If so, ask God's forgiveness and build a new biblical belief.

FIVE

PROSPERITY PRINCIPLES

If you are willing and obedient,
you shall eat the good of the land.

Isaiah 1:19

There is a young businessman in our church named Eric whom I would classify as a dreamer. He believes he is to do great things for the Kingdom of God and that God has empowered him to create wealth. But, as is often the case, his dream has hit a few snags along the way.

After a particularly prosperous season, it seemed as if his flow of income had come to an abrupt halt. Resources had dried up and he was in trouble. He came to me for prayer and counsel.

I have known Eric most of his life, but I still asked the questions: "Have you been faithful in your tithes and offerings? Have your business dealings been righteous [meaning he was not taking shortcuts that compromised his integrity]? Have you paid your bills?" He was able to answer *yes* to all these questions. So what was the problem?

I have found that, when times like this occur, it is often the enemy's assault—not only on our finances, but on our calling as well. Eric was called to be a Kingdom entrepreneur, gifted not only to generate finances but to operate in wisdom and strategies that produce results. This crisis was shaking Eric, even trying to break him.

We must understand, as I noted earlier, that the enemy is a legalist and will look for spiritual legal ground to forge his attack. For this reason I sensed God saying for me to ask Eric to seek the Lord regarding five lessons God was teaching him during this crisis, so he could repent and remove every accusation against him and his business. We prayed together that God would show him prophetically every area that needed alignment, so he could decree that what the enemy had stolen from him would return sevenfold.

The Lord showed Eric several areas he needed to reinforce. And as he and his wife prayed and repented over these and other areas, things began to shift. The first shift was in his faith. Instead of feeling hopeless and overwhelmed, he remembered who God had called him to be and the gifts he had been given to accomplish great things. Hope began to rise. It released his faith, and his faith began to release miracles.

And as Eric employed these principles, his business began to turn around. Then it skyrocketed. Within a matter of two weeks from his point of crisis, his commission-based business went from almost no listings to nearly one hundred million dollars' worth of listings. Immediately he began to see contracts being signed and commissions being paid.

I had been preaching on the "third-day anointing" of the resurrection life of Jesus Christ—how throughout Scripture God intervened in human affairs on the third day, and how this anointing for resurrection power touches every area of our lives. Eric grabbed hold of this message and began decreeing life to his business. As a sign of God's favor and as a response to his faith, his first new commission check came in at 3 p.m. on the third day of the third month for $30,000! It was also his third new lead that generated the sale. God loves to confirm His Word with signs following! Eric saw once again that biblical principles produce powerful results.

In this chapter we are going to identify and explore some of these principles.

Turning the Curse to Blessing

As many of us pray for revival throughout the earth, we are believing that God will bring about a harvest of souls.

One of the definitions of the verb *to revive* is "to recover from financial depression."[1] Clearly it takes resources to carry out the Great Commission and for believers to implement their God-given vision.

As a matter of fact, one of the meanings of the prefix *pro* in the word *provision* is "earlier than" or "prior to";[2] and the etymology of the word *provision* comes from the Latin, "to see ahead."[3] Before God gives you a vision, He already has provision to fulfill the vision. The enemy loves to cut off supply lines to prevent Kingdom business from taking place, and he gets us to buy in to his limitations through lies and deceit. But God wants to turn things around.

This book is not about money but about taking authority over every work of the enemy. One of the areas the enemy steals from people most often is in their finances. Sometimes it is a purely spiritual attack against the righteous. At other times we, like Eric, need to examine our perspective and principles regarding money to ensure that these are lining up with biblical expectations. Scripture says people are destroyed for lack of knowledge (see Hosea 4:6). We cannot confront the thief if we are unwilling to examine how he tries to get us out of alignment with God through our ignorance or disregard of spiritual principles.

In this chapter we will explore common areas of financial misalignment with Scripture that open the door to the thief. These ungodly beliefs often cause us to miss out on the blessings of God. It is important to replace ungodly mindsets and belief systems with biblical principles that unlock unlimited resources for our assignments.

God longs to turn the curse to a blessing because He loves us (see Deuteronomy 23:5). As we align ourselves with the Word of God, we see the Lord rise up and "rebuke the devourer" for us (see Malachi 3:11). Then He delights in restoring all the enemy has stolen. It is a one-two punch against the darkness!

The Source of All Faith

Every principle of our faith must be grounded in the Word of God. In Romans Paul encourages us about our faith:

> What does it say? "The word is near you, in your mouth and in your heart" (that is, the word of faith which we preach): that if you confess with your mouth the Lord Jesus and believe in your heart that God has raised Him from the dead, you will be saved. . . . So then faith comes by hearing, and hearing by the word of God.
>
> Romans 10:8–9, 17

Every other principle of faith operates off these basic principles. First, we must have faith in God and believe in our hearts. How do we gain that faith? By hearing the Word of God. Second, we must speak or decree what we believe. And third, we must agree with the Word through our actions, since faith without works is dead (see James 2:26). In laying strong biblical principles for prosperity, then, let me encourage you to study the Word of God for yourself.

Mine is by no means an exhaustive list of prosperity principles to employ. I believe, however, that these are some of the most important ones in confronting the thief. Also, please understand that you cannot pick and choose which of these principles to follow. You must incorporate each one as found in the Word of God. Jesus came to redeem us from every curse, and break every chain that hinders us from living full lives in Christ and fulfilling His call on our lives.

Breaking the Inner Vow of Poverty

These principles have changed my life. As I mentioned earlier, I struggled personally with a poverty mindset. This was not because I was raised poor. My family was middle class and my parents budgeted carefully, so I never remember lacking anything. Rather, my poverty mindset came because someone once suggested that I was going into the ministry to become a "money-grabbing preacher." Oh my! So at the age of sixteen, I made an inner vow that I would rather have nothing than ever be in a position to be accused of being in ministry for money.

And I am here to report, the vow worked, because we had nothing.

This "vow" may sound noble, sacrificial, and spiritual, and it did reflect my heart. But after a careful study of the Word of God, I became convinced of God's heart for me through Scriptures like 3 John 2: "Beloved, I pray that you may prosper in all things and be in health, just as your soul prospers." The Holy Spirit spoke to me and confronted me with having rejected the Father's blessings. I had to repent and renew my

103

mind, breaking my inner vow of poverty and the enemy's legal hold against me.

That worked as well! It was as if the windows of heaven were opened to me, and God began to pour out provision and blessings on our family. He broke every curse and brought divine recovery into my life.

Principles for Prosperity

Here are nine principles from Scripture that have changed my life.

1. God Delights in Prospering His Children

Scripture is full of passages regarding God's heart for His people to prosper in every area of their lives. In Joshua 1:8, God directly ties the understanding of His Word with our ability to prosper:

> This Book of the Law shall not depart from your mouth, but you shall meditate in it day and night, that you may observe to do according to all that is written in it. For then you will make your way prosperous, and then you will have good success.

God wanted to set His children up to prosper and have good success. And He delighted in blessing Abraham—who "believed God" (Romans 4:3)—with abundance. He was one of the wealthiest men on earth in his day. God said to him in Genesis 12:

> I will bless you and make your name great; and you shall be a blessing. I will bless those who bless you, and I will curse him who curses you; and in you all the families of the earth shall be blessed.
>
> Genesis 12:2–3

Deuteronomy 8:18 displays God's heart for Israel as they were coming out of captivity into the Promised Land:

> You shall remember the LORD your God, for it is He who gives you power to get wealth, that He may establish His covenant which He swore to your fathers, as it is this day.

The word *get* in Hebrew is *asah*, which means to make, to bring forth, or to procure.[4] God delighted in blessing Israel, even giving her power to *asah* wealth. Many in the Body of Christ are waiting on God to bless them, as though resources will fall out of heaven. Rather, God has blessed us with His own creative power to create wealth. Instead of a wealth-transfer mindset, God want us to have a wealth-creation mentality.

In Proverbs, a book of wisdom and godly principles, God makes promises to those who follow His precepts:

> With me are riches and honor, enduring wealth and prosperity. My fruit is better than fine gold; what I yield surpasses choice silver. I walk in the way of righteousness, along the paths of justice, bestowing wealth on those who love me and making their treasuries full.
>
> Proverbs 8:18–21 NIV1984

God delights in freely dispensing righteous wisdom for us to experience His goodness as He makes our treasuries full.

To be clear, one can have "full treasuries" of joy, peace, and righteousness without having a full bank account. The first-century disciples were willing to forsake all earthly wealth to follow Christ. And many believers throughout the earth today are suffering lack due to religious persecution, war, and societal oppression. This certainly does not mean God does not love them or care about their circumstances. But even in harsh conditions, God delights in providing for His people and filling the treasure chests of their lives with expressions of His amazing goodness, which cannot always be measured monetarily. God always finds ways to bless and enrich those who walk in His ways.

2. Jesus Ministered to Both Rich and Poor

I had a conversation with someone once who defended living in poverty as a more spiritual way to live, citing Jesus' own lack of houses, lands, or material possessions. It is true that Jesus said, "Foxes have holes and birds of the air have nests, but the Son of Man has nowhere to lay His head" (Matthew 8:20). He spent a great portion of His ministry tending to those from the lower class of society. He touched the lives of poor fishermen, prostitutes, widows, and orphans.

Yet Jesus also ministered to the rich and influential. He often spoke with Sadducees, Pharisees, and the Sanhedrin. He talked with the rich young ruler and the Roman centurion, and counted as His followers men of renown such as Nicodemus and Joseph of Arimathea (see Luke 7:1–5; John 3:1–21; 19:38). He attended feasts, dined with the rich, and even received costly gifts from those who loved Him (see Luke 5:29–32; 7:36–39; John 2:1–2; 12:1–3). Many of His parables dealt with the responsibility to invest and make a profit (see Matthew 25:14–30; Luke 19:11–27).

He also taught His disciples about sacrifice, saying they would be required to give things up for the sake of the Gospel. Yet even in this, He promised that they would "receive a hundredfold now in this time . . . and in the age to come, eternal life" (Mark 10:30).

Second Corinthians 8:9 says, "You know the grace of our Lord Jesus Christ, that though He was rich, yet for your sakes He became poor, that you through His poverty might become rich." These words were written by the apostle Paul as he exhorted the Corinthian church about giving—even in their need—so they could become rich.

Obviously Christ came to give us an abundance of spiritual blessings that far exceed anything material. The word *rich* in the Greek, however, *plouteo*, means to become wealthy or to be increased with goods.[5] It also means to have an abundance of outward possessions, to be richly supplied.[6] Even though we can never allow material blessings to outshine the depth of our spiritual blessings, we must be aware that God delights in blessing us in every area.

3. We Must Be Willing to Work

Work was God's idea. When He placed Adam in the Garden, before the Fall, God gave him work assignments in tending the Garden, naming the animals, and being productive. God gave instructions about work long before He gave instructions about worship. Work can be a form of worship when all we do is unto the Lord.

The apostle Paul worked and earned a living by his trade of tentmaking (see Acts 18:3). He exhorted the Thessalonians "that you also aspire to lead a quiet life, to mind your own business, and to work with your own hands, as we commanded you" (1 Thessalonians 4:11). And again, "If anyone will not work, neither shall he eat" (2 Thessalonians 3:10).

I knew a Bible college student who "by faith" quit his job and dedicated himself to praying eight hours a day. He did not consult his roommates, nor did they agree. This young man had a good heart, but he was violating a biblical principle that would actually block and prevent his provision.

Work is not unholy. It is a command from the Lord. If we want to be blessed, we must ask God to bless the work of our hands (see Psalm 90:17).

4. We Must Not Make Money an Idol

An old saying goes, "You can have money as long as money does not have you." We can see this in Paul's exhortation to Timothy that "the love of money is the root of all evil" (1 Timothy 6:10 KJV). In *The Passion Translation* the whole verse reads:

> Loving money is a root of all evils. Some people run after it so much that they have given up their faith. Craving more money pushes them away from the faith into error, compounding misery in their lives!

Notice, money is not evil; it is the love of money that leads us astray. So don't let money steal your worship.

Jesus made the correlation between our love of God and our loyalty to mammon, by confronting this false god directly:

> No servant can serve two masters; for either he will hate the one and love the other, or else he will be loyal to the one and despise the other. You cannot serve God and mammon.
>
> Luke 16:13

Mammon is commonly considered to mean money, material wealth, avarice, and riches. Mammon personified, however, is thought to be the demon or false god of greed, and is associated with evil, corruption, and the immoral acquisition of wealth. Mammon is similar to Baal in the Old Testament, the god of wealth and riches. We must never find ourselves in a place of worshiping or loving money more than we worship and love God.[7]

Os Hillman, a popular teacher on business, wealth, and Kingdom living, has this to say:

> The New Testament contains 2,084 verses dealing with money and finance. Sixteen of Jesus' thirty-eight parables deal with

money. The reason Jesus spoke so much about money was because He was always trying to see where a person's loyalty resided. "For where your treasure is, there your heart will be also" (Matt 6:21 NKJV). He said a person could not serve two masters. Instead, he will love one but hate the other. Many people believe money is synonymous with mammon. This is incorrect. Mammon is an Aramaic demonic spirit that was worshipped as a false god by the Philistines. Mammon desires to be worshipped, have influence, and control people's lives to require love and devotion through the use of money. Money is simply the instrument by which mammon seeks to have power.[8]

Pastor Jimmy Evans says this regarding mammon:

Mammon promises us those things that only God can give—security, significance, identity, independence, power, and freedom. Mammon tells us that it can insulate us from life's problems and that money is the answer to every situation.[9]

A poverty mindset is unscriptural, but so are mentalities of materialism and greed. They can be two sides of the same coin.

So how does one defeat wrong desires for money or things? Give. I have found that people who are true givers have an easier time keeping their priorities straight. Lack of money will test your heart, but so will receiving abundance. It is not about the money; it is about our heart toward it.

Jesus challenged the priorities of His disciples in Matthew 6:33: "Seek first the kingdom of God and His righteousness, and all these things shall be added to you." Seeking Him must always come first. Every material blessing must be secondary to the call of the Kingdom. If you hope to do great things for God, you must understand that sacrifice is part of the journey. Embrace sacrifice and be willing to give up everything if God asks, without partnering with a poverty mindset.

5. Prosperity Brings Kingdom Influence

When Tom and I were young in ministry and struggling to make ends meet, my mother used to help us do our taxes. She saw how much we made each year and wondered how we could survive. She also wondered how we were so happy, living fulfilling lives regardless of our financial state. She used to say, "You guys are the richest poor people I know!"

While it is an incredible blessing to have had grace during those years, I came to realize that God wanted much more for us. He longed to bless us and increase our influence in our community. Ecclesiastes 9:16 says, "Wisdom is better than strength. Nevertheless the poor man's wisdom is despised, and his words are not heard."

Jesus told us to use worldly wealth to create influence:

> Remember this: The sons of darkness interact more wisely than the sons of light. Use the wealth of this world to demonstrate your friendship with God by winning friends and blessing others. Then, when it runs out, your generosity will provide you with an eternal reward. The one who faithfully manages the little he has been given will be promoted and trusted with greater responsibilities.
>
> Luke 16:8–10 TPT

Tom and I needed to take the limits off God. He wanted to bless us and, in so doing, increase our influence. We had bought into a lie from the enemy causing us to live below the poverty line. We needed to stop being afraid of the blessings of the Lord. Proverbs 10:22 says, "The blessing of the LORD makes one rich, and He adds no sorrow with it."

ALLOWING GOD TO BLESS US

Tom and I were believing God for a new house. We were living in a mobile home at the time and not making much money as we pioneered in ministry. But I longed for a more permanent home, one built on a real foundation, with space enough for our growing family. We had received prophecies about that home. So Tom drew up a set of plans and we began to dream.

One weekend a prophet came to our church and said, "The Lord shows me a set of house plans. But He is not pleased. You have to make it bigger."

We could not even afford the modest home we were praying about! But in obedience Tom drew up another set of plans that was fifty percent larger.

The next month another prophet came through and said much what the previous prophet had. Once again he told us to make the house plans bigger. Wow! Bigger? We were definitely not going to be able to afford this house! But in obedience Tom made it bigger. Now our plans were double what he had drawn initially.

The next month God sent another prophet. This one said, "I see a set of house plans, and the Lord says He is pleased!" (*Whew!*) He added, "Now I will release money for you to build that house, and you will be amazed at My blessing." At the time we had no money saved for our house since we were in a building project at the church and sowing heavily into that. That night the prophet added, "When I give you money for your house, woe unto you if you put it into the building fund."

That night a woman approached us with a large check, saying that the Lord had told her to bless us, but she had prayed that God would send a prophet so we would use the money for our home and not put it into the building fund. God has such a sense of humor!

We ended up building our new home that year. God blessed us through personal gifts, family gifts, and investments, so that within four months of this prophetic word, we had more than twenty percent of the construction cost, so we could get a loan.

It was a miracle! But it began by our hearing the voice of God and taking the limits off, to allow Him to bless us.

This breakthrough brought us into a whole new place of influence in our life and community. While we lived in a mobile home, our community viewed us as transient. When we built a house, we were viewed as permanent members of the community. Not only that, but our breakthrough became a blessing to others as well. Ours was the first home built on our street in a brand-new subdivision. After our home was finished, many of our elders and leaders also had faith to step out and build their homes. The principles of faith we learned on this journey broke the mindset of limitation off our lives and caused increase to come—not just financially, but for greater influence for the Kingdom of God through our lives and ministry.

TAKING THE LIMITS OFF

Maybe you are reading this thinking that you want God to bless you, and that you have no issues with a poverty mindset. But is there any area in which you are limiting yourself or God? Is there any area in which you have put a limitation on your God-ordained vision because of how much it would cost to fully obey God?

God wants to take believers from simply working a job to occupying a position of influence. He wants to make you a leader in your workplace and community. And yes, He desires to bring increase into your financial situation. It is time for us to raise our expectations, knowing it will result in greater influence for the Kingdom of God in the earth.

6. Prosperity Is Activated through Giving

In the previous chapter we addressed the issue of giving God a tithe, or ten percent, of all our increase. But there are many other forms of giving that also rebuke the devourer, break off curses, and release the blessing of God in our lives.

We must understand and practice the biblical law of sowing and reaping—offerings we give above and beyond our tithe. We see this illustrated in Genesis 26, when there was a terrible famine in the land. The Lord told Isaac to stay in that land and sow seed.

> Then Isaac sowed in that land, and reaped in the same year a hundredfold; and the LORD blessed him. The man began to prosper, and continued prospering until he became very prosperous.
>
> Genesis 26:12–13

This was faith in action. There are at least four ways we can demonstrate it.

THE FREEWILL OFFERING

Isaac's obedience to the Lord in sowing seed brought not only his prosperity but his influence with his Philistine neighbors, who envied his miraculous supply in the time of famine (see Genesis 26:14–33).

If you are experiencing lack or famine in your life, consider planting a seed. And be sure to do it "bountifully" and joyfully, as "God loves a cheerful giver" (2 Corinthians 9:6–7). The seed of your freewill offering becomes a pathway to prosperity and advancement.

FIRSTFRUITS

Proverbs 3:9–10 instructs us to "honor the LORD with your possessions, and with the firstfruits of all your increase; so your barns will be filled with plenty, and your vats will overflow with new wine." Firstfruits from the harvest were brought to the house of the Lord and given to the priest—the giving of the first portion of what was reaped.

Today it may mean the giving of a portion of the first paycheck of the year or month, or the giving of a portion of a bonus you receive—an expression of generosity for all the things the Lord blesses you with. It is different from the tithe, which is the giving of ten percent and required to be brought to the house of God.

Firstfruits celebrate through an offering a time when your hard work has paid off, and they are often given directly to the priest or spiritual leader. We turn to the Lord with gratitude and honor Him with the fruit of our increase, giving Him our best gift without guilt or obligation (see Exodus 34:26; Nehemiah 10:37; Ezekiel 44:30).

ALMS FOR THE POOR

A third type of giving is "alms," or gifts for the poor. Proverbs 28:27 says, "He who gives to the poor will not lack." Again in Proverbs 19:17: "He who has pity on the poor lends to the LORD, and He will pay back what he has given." Giving alms should be part of our giving plan.

The tithe, you see, connects us to our covenant with God. Our offerings connect us to our potential for increase. Firstfruits connect us to our leaders, to honor them. And alms connect us to the heart of God and compassion.

OBEDIENT GIVING, EXTRAVAGANT GOD

While I was breaking out of a poverty mindset and learning about the law of sowing and reaping, God impressed on me to give a ring to a pastor's wife who was having a challenging time. It was not an expensive ring, but my husband had saved up to give it to me during our early years of financial struggle. But I felt that God wanted to bless this woman, and He spoke to me that my giving away something meaningful would help break the spirit of poverty in my life. So I asked Tom's permission and he agreed.

We were at a conference with more than a thousand people. I left the service and went to find the woman. I took her to a private corner in the building where no one else could see, and gave her the ring as a sign of God's love and covenant with her.

She wept, sensing that God saw her struggles and heard her prayers, and she said how my gift encouraged her. Never underestimate the power of a sacrificial gift to demonstrate God's heart to someone!

We hugged, and I began to make my way back to my seat. But first I stopped by the ladies' room. When I came out, a woman I did not know was waiting for me with tears in her eyes and a ring in her hand. She said the Lord had spoken to her that morning to give me this ring—which was of much greater value than the one I had just given away. It was to be a sign, she said, of His love and covenant with me, and how much He longed to bless me.

Wow, I did not expect that! I cried, hugged, and thanked the woman, and continued to my seat.

As I stepped into the hallway leading to the meeting room, another woman I did not know was waiting for me with a smile on her face and a ring in her hand. She said the same thing the previous woman had said, placed the ring on my hand, and hugged me.

What was going on?

As I stepped into the meeting hall, another woman was waiting to bless me with a ring.

And another.

And another.

Keep in mind that no one had seen me give my little ring away. But God saw.

Before I made it back to my seat, I had been given seven rings by women I did not know but who felt God had spoken to them to do so. He was showing me once again His extravagant nature and how deeply He wanted to bless me as part of His love and covenant with me. My giving had unlocked the extravagant blessings of the Lord, which make rich and add no sorrow.

I have since blessed others with six of the seven rings. The seventh is a reminder of the day the spirit of poverty broke off my life—not just because I gave but because I was willing to receive God's extravagant gifts with joy.

As you read this, ask the Lord if you have any lingering poverty mentality putting limits on your blessings. The thief will try to keep you bound in poverty or greed. One of the ways to break free is by giving something meaningful away to someone else.

Once Tom and I gave a financial gift to the richest man in our church. It was only a few hundred dollars; and when the Lord spoke this to us, we did not understand why we were to give it to him. Then the Lord said, *He does not need your seed, but you need his soil. Plant in prosperous ground.*

Our recipient actually cried, saying that no one had ever given him anything; he was always the giver. It truly touched his heart. And beyond that, it was an interesting lesson for us all, that at times our seed is not planted just to fill someone's need but also to communicate God's love and care to that individual. Besides, the rich soil of this man's prosperous life became a place where our seed could multiply back to us in blessing, in many ways.

Perhaps God would have you sow something of value into someone else's need. See a need and plant a seed. Or perhaps your gift will go to someone you do not suspect needs it. The most important thing is to be willing to be a blessing on every occasion and to be obedient to follow God's voice. It will change your life—and maybe someone else's besides.

7. Prosperity Is Empowered through Decreeing over the Seed

Once the Lord said to me, *Jane, you and Tom are great sowers, but you are terrible reapers.* As I asked Him what He meant, He explained that a farmer does not just go throw seed out in a field and come back months later to reap. No, the farmer tends the seed and watches over it. I asked the Lord how to tend the seed, and He said we needed to make decrees over our seed, pray in the Spirit, and raise our expectations—otherwise the robber would come like a bird and pluck up the seed.

Matthew 7:7 says, "Ask, and it will be given to you; seek, and you will find; knock, and it will be opened to you." This is a proactive positioning of faith. It is not enough to hope for things; we need to learn to ask and expect and be specific.

So Tom and I made a list of every seed we had sown over the previous six months. We repented of our passive positioning of sowing seed and then just waiting to see if anything changed. We began to pray in the Spirit and decree the Word of God over the seed. Psalm 118:25, for example, says, "Send now prosperity."

As we prayed and decreed, we saw things begin to shift and provision begin to flow. This principle of praying in our supernatural language and decreeing over the seed made us partners with God.

8. We Are Blessed to Be a Blessing

God told Abraham He would bless him and then make him a blessing. This should be the heart of every believer—to use our blessings to become a blessing to others. God longs to bless His people, but He is also serious about our keeping a right heart in the midst of blessing. Prosperity must be pure.

9. Forgiveness Is Part of God's Plan

Maybe you have experienced being robbed by the thief. I think we all have. It is easy to think in spiritual terms and forget that we have a responsibility to forgive those who may have partnered with the enemy in robbing us. We must practice the spiritual principle of forgiveness toward those who have cost us money, done us wrong, and robbed us of time, joy, and vision.

Perhaps you have had some bad experiences with a business partner, a past spouse, a parent, or another family member. Forgive that person. Release that person from any judgment you may hold against him or her. Perhaps someone has borrowed money from you and never paid it back. Forgive that person and, if God asks you to, forgive the debt. Take that debt into the court of heaven and ask God to bring recovery.

Some may have felt like Job, who lost houses, children, possessions, even his health. Even his wife gave him terrible advice to basically curse God and die. But in Job 42:10–12 it says, "The LORD restored Job's losses when he prayed for his friends. Indeed the LORD gave Job twice as much as he had before." *The Message* says it this way: "After Job had interceded for his friends, GOD restored his fortune—and then doubled it!"

Job received double for his trouble because he blessed those who cursed him. We should do the same.

A DECREE TO TAKE BACK YOUR BLESSING

[Speak this aloud in faith!] *Because I am a child of God, all His blessings are mine. I can push forward and break out of limitation. I can receive anointed strategies for success. I can have peace and health along the way, and I can succeed in all I put my hands to do.*

Because I am a child of God, He is looking for ways to bless me, so that He can make me a blessing. Opportunities are mine. Open doors are mine. Wisdom and strategy are mine. I am anointed to create wealth.

I renounce every inner vow of poverty or lack, and I repent of limiting God's desire to bless me. The blessings of the Lord make rich and do not add any sorrow at all. My seeds will prosper and bring increase. Blessing and prosperity are mine. I am blessed and highly favored by the Lord Most High. All the enemy has stolen from me, he must return to me double, or even seven times the value. I receive full recovery from the Lord. And I am blessed to be a blessing, in Jesus' name.

ACTIVATION: FILE A ROBBERY REPORT

If you came home to discover that your home had been burglarized, you would probably call the police. The police would then have you file a robbery report to detail all that had been stolen. It is the first step in getting your possessions back.

This is similar to filing your Writ of Replevin, but it may resonate differently with you. So let's do this together.

1. Make a list of everything the enemy has stolen from you. Do not just include material or monetary things; also include things like time, energy, health, joy, family, etc.
2. Find several Scriptures to stand on, such as Exodus 22:7, "If the thief is found, he shall pay double," or Isaiah 61:7, "Instead of your shame you shall have double honor."
3. Forgive those who have wronged you. Forgive in your heart and speak the words out loud, which releases those people from either judgment or debt.

4. Bring your robbery report to the throne of God and make your appeal to the King, to receive a return (see 2 Kings 8:5–6).

5. Sow a seed and make a decree. It could be something like the decree above.

QUESTIONS TO CONSIDER

1. While reading the Principles for Prosperity in this chapter, were you able to identify any areas that challenged your biblical understanding of wealth? Which area challenged you most?

2. Can you identify any areas of your life that could be considered loving, worshiping, serving, or aligning with mammon more than with God? If so, repent of these areas and search the Word of God for Scriptures that bring these areas into proper alignment with biblical truth.

3. Can you identify any area in which you may need to "take the limits off" in your quest for God's best in your life?

SIX

TAKING BACK OUR PURPOSE

Many are the plans in a person's heart, but it is the LORD's purpose that prevails.

Proverbs 19:21 NIV

When I was sixteen years old, I heard the voice of the Lord for the first time as I prayed. He said to me, *Jane, the plans you have made for your life are not the plans I have made for your life. Instead of going to that college, I will send you to Bible college. There you will meet a man and you will marry young. I will thrust you into ministry and you will travel the nations of the earth. Sometimes he will preach and sometimes you will preach, for I have called you to be a ministry team.*

I had never heard of a woman preacher before. I certainly had no concept of a husband-and-wife team in ministry. So I asked the Lord, "Can You show me someone doing what I will be doing, so I know what You are talking about?" He responded, *There is no one currently doing what you will be doing, for I will be doing a new thing.*

I was excited about the call of God on my life! I ran immediately to my denominational pastor to share this news with him. He patted me on the back and said, "Girlie, that wasn't the voice of God, because women don't preach." I walked away confused.

The following week I was asked to leave that church, because they believed me to be a danger to the body with my crazy claims that God had spoken to me. I was devastated. They had been my church family for two years, since I was born again.

I had lessons to learn in processing heartbreak, forgiveness, and not becoming bitter, which was a first step in pursuing my calling.

Two weeks later I was visiting another church. This was a Spirit-filled church, and the pastor, Pastor Eddie, pointed his finger at me before he preached and said, "Young lady, God wants you to know that you will preach the Word and signs will follow."

That was my first prophecy from a person, and it confirmed what God had spoken to me. I made plans to attend Christ For The Nations Institute in Dallas. There I met my husband, Tom, my first night on campus. We were married two years later and immediately planted a church. A few years later we started another church in Florida, which we have been pastoring for almost forty years. Sometimes he preaches and sometimes I preach, because we are a team. We have traveled to more than 65 nations.

But the early years were a struggle for me as a woman in ministry. I had to make choices to obey and follow God, even when it was not easy.

When God places a call on your life, you will have to contend for that call, because the enemy will do everything in his power to stop you from fulfilling your destiny. He will work hard to get you out of proper positioning and compromise your obedience. In truth, the enemy will let you have all the material things—money, houses, possessions, and more—as long as he can get you to give up your high calling in Christ and compromise your walk. In doing so, the thief will have robbed you of one of the most important things in life: God's prophetic purpose.

A Price to Pay

Psalm 29:4 declares, "The voice of the LORD is powerful." This is a simple yet profound statement. The word of the Lord changed my life. You may have had your life changed, too, by something the Lord has spoken to you, either through a prophet or prophetic minister, through His Word, through a vision or dream, or even through His still, small voice.

One word from God changes everything.

Yet throughout Scripture we see that the prophetic promise shedding light on God's created purpose for an individual was the very thing that presented the greatest challenge. Abraham was called "father of nations," yet he had to wait a long time before producing his first child. Joseph was given dreams of ruling over a people, yet he was betrayed by his brothers, sold into slavery, accused falsely, and thrown into prison, before he was brought before Pharaoh and made his right-hand man, ruling the nation of Egypt. David was a shepherd boy, the youngest in his family, told by the prophet Samuel that he would be king over Israel. Yet for the next thirteen years or so, he had to run from King Saul, who sought to kill him. All the while he honored God and the very king who wanted him dead.

Just because God speaks a thing does not guarantee that its fulfillment will be easy. There is always a price to pay to fulfill your prophetic purpose. There will be choices to make, people to forgive, and finances to sacrifice. But keeping your heart fixed on God's prophesied purpose will hold you steady through the challenging times.

This is what focused Jesus as He suffered, bled, and died. Hebrews 12:2 tells us that "for the joy that was set before Him [He] endured the cross, despising the shame." What was that joy? We, His Bride, were His joy, enabling Him to endure such pain and suffering. As we keep our eyes on Him and all He has spoken to us, we will receive the same grace to endure and overcome all things.

My spiritual father, Bishop Bill Hamon, loves to say, "God is more interested in making the man than the mighty ministry." This is God's order of priority. He is not afraid to test and try our hearts along our journey of fulfilling the call. Ultimately He wants our character to be able to carry our calling. The test is not a punishment but a preparation for fulfillment of the prophetic promise.

Reformation or Rebellion?

After the conquest of Canaan, God set up a governmental system of judges who ruled the land. Samuel was one of the greatest judges and prophets in the Old Testament. As he assumed his role, the Philistines were ravaging the land. God's strategy was for Samuel to call the people to repent, turn back to God, and destroy all their idols. If they would do these things, God would fight for them.

The people responded, and God did vanquish the Philistine enemy that had robbed Israel of land. God brought her into a time of peace and prosperity as she recovered all the enemy had stolen. First Samuel 7:14 tells us:

> Then the cities which the Philistines had taken from Israel were restored to Israel, from Ekron to Gath; and Israel recovered its

territory from the hands of the Philistines. Also there was peace between Israel and the Amorites.

God is anointing us to recover our territory, too, personal territory as well as regions and nations. Yet as we know from Scripture, the Philistines remained a threat to the future destiny of the Israelites, depending on how they positioned their hearts with God.

Under Samuel's leadership, they enjoyed one of their greatest times of blessing. In modern terms, the land was ripe for revival. It seemed their prayers were being answered, hearts were turned back to God, and breakthroughs abounded. But in this time of blessing, they became comfortable, complacent, and dissatisfied with God and His ways. They sought change. In the moment that God wanted change in the form of reformation—a new season of profound established victory and oneness with Him—they chose rebellion.

In seasons of change, reformers turn toward God and His purposes. Rebels turn away and usually take others with them.

Israel cried out rebelliously for a king to rule over them so they would be like all the other nations, having a great king to lead them into battle. God did not intend for them to be like the other nations, but to be separate and distinct. But the Israelites decided they knew best. God considered this a great wickedness. Nevertheless He answered the cry of His people, instructing Samuel to give them a king, "for they have not rejected you, but they have rejected Me, that I should not reign over them" (1 Samuel 8:7).

Samuel warned the people that the king they wanted would take from them their children, land, crops, and livestock. They would become the servants of the king they were choosing, rather than the servants of God. Still they chose their own way instead of God's.

At times the things we think we need to succeed or to fulfill our promise can become the very things that enslave us. Our own choices become tools of the thief to keep us from our prophetic purpose. This is true for individuals and, as we see with Israel, entire nations as well.

The United States, and many other nations as well, have known the blessings and abundance of God—I believe in large part due to the Judeo-Christian values that have underpinned our societal structure. We have been a nation of reformers, change-makers. We do not have a sinless history, but God has shed His grace on us. But in our blessings, we have grown complacent and rebellious, saying that we do not want the God of the Bible to rule us. We ourselves know what is best for the destiny of our nation, we say. And our independence has led us into bondage. Instead of choosing a giving, blessing God, our nation has chosen an enemy that takes from us—our families, our purity, our destiny of greatness.

The only answer is repentance. God stands ready to heal our land when we turn from our wicked ways (see 2 Chronicles 7:14). There is no other way forward.

Saul's Prophetic Purpose

During the time of the rebellion of Israel, after she demanded a king, the Lord told Samuel about a young, handsome man named Saul from the tribe of Benjamin. Samuel was to anoint him commander over Israel, "that he may save My people from the hand of the Philistines" (1 Samuel 9:16).

What a powerful prophetic purpose! Although Israel's request was made in rebellion to God, Saul was God's choice.

Saul met Samuel while he was searching for his father's lost donkeys. The prophet told him of God's plan for his life to be king over Israel, then outlined a series of events that would take place to confirm all he said. One of the things to occur was that Saul would meet a company of prophets, that the Spirit of the Lord would come upon him, and that he, too, would prophesy and "be turned into another man" (1 Samuel 10:6).

Saul had a radical experience with the Spirit of God. As he met up with the prophets, he, too, began to prophesy. This incredible encounter confirmed all that Samuel had spoken to him.

There is something about getting around prophetic people that causes the Spirit of God to be stirred up within a person, enabling one also to hear God's voice.

But God put conditions on Saul's reign. If Saul and the people would turn their hearts to God and fear Him, remembering all He had done for them, God would bless them. But if not, He said, "You shall be swept away, both you and your king" (1 Samuel 12:25).

Some today believe that if God has spoken a promise over them, it will undoubtedly come to pass. But success and blessing are not automatic just because God has spoken them. They are predicated on obedience and heart positioning before God. In this instance with Israel, God was clear about the conditions. At other times a prophetic word may speak of destiny, promise, and blessing without stating conditions. Regardless, prophecies come to pass only as believers stay in obedience and alignment with God's purposes.

Saul was anointed king and enjoyed some early victories during his reign. The first enemy he had to contend with was the Philistines. But wait! Didn't God give Israel victory and recovery of land from the Philistines? Yes. But the very act of requesting a king demonstrated that the people had turned their hearts away from trusting God. So their old enemy showed up, ready to do battle once again. It is not just about getting free; it is about staying free!

The name *Philistine* comes from a root word in Hebrew that means to roll in the dust or to wallow in self.[1] I have told our congregation many times that I am more afraid of myself than I am of the devil. I am the one who gets me out of alignment with God. I am the one who falls into the trap of pride and independence. I am the one who resists the ways of faith.

It is easy to blame the devil for anything that goes wrong in our lives. While it is true that the enemy is always looking for inroads into our lives to tempt us, lead us astray, and then rob us, it is our own self-will that falls into the trap, making us easy prey for the devourer. This is what happened with Saul.

The Fall of Saul

The fall of Saul occurred in two phases: first, during his fight with the Philistines, and then with Agag of the Amalekites, the thieves.

Illegitimate Sacrifice

In the first phase, we find Saul in 1 Samuel 13 unwisely picking a fight with the Philistines, who greatly outnumbered Israel and pushed them back in battle. As a result, the Israelites ran and hid out in caves, holes, and pits. Samuel had told Saul that he would come in seven days and offer sacrifices, and to wait for him; yet Samuel did not come on time. When Saul saw the people in distress, in his fear and pride he offered a burnt offering to the Lord, which was forbidden, since only a priest or judge could offer such an offering. As soon as it was done, Samuel showed up, saying, "What have you done?"

This was a great sin before God. But the real trouble was when Samuel confronted Saul with his sin and Saul refused to take personal responsibility, blaming first the people for scattering, then Samuel for not showing up on time, and then the enemy. All these "compelled" him to offer the illegitimate sacrifice. His excuse of "the devil made me do it" did not appease Samuel or God. Fear, insecurity, people-pleasing, and disobedience set Saul up for a fall.

Had he repented and taken responsibility for his sin, perhaps he would not have heard Samuel's next words:

> You have done foolishly. You have not kept the commandment of the LORD your God, which He commanded you. For now the LORD would have established your kingdom over Israel forever. But now your kingdom shall not continue. The LORD has sought for Himself a man after His own heart . . . because you have not kept what the LORD commanded you.
>
> 1 Samuel 13:13–14

Thank God we are not living under the Old Testament law, but under New Testament grace. Thank God one mistake does not erase an entire destiny. But God is serious about obedience as well as heart positioning. Saul was so filled with pride that he could not see or admit his sin.

We cannot think that we can fulfill the things of the Spirit while following our flesh.

The Agag Trap

In the second phase of Saul's fall, we see a similar situation in the Israelites' battle against the Amalekites, the robbers. God spoke prophetically to Saul through Samuel:

> Thus says the LORD of hosts: "I will punish Amalek for what he did to Israel, how he ambushed him on the way when he came up from Egypt. Now go and attack Amalek, and utterly destroy all that they have, and do not spare them. But kill both

man and woman, infant and nursing child, ox and sheep, camel and donkey."

1 Samuel 15:2–3

This was a harsh mission for Saul to carry out, but the prophetic directives were clear. They demonstrate God's utter hatred for the robber, the one who ambushed His people. God is impressing on us once again His call to arms against the robber, and instructing us to have no mercy in punishing our spiritual foe.

Yet Saul failed to execute the word. He decided he knew a better way than what God had prescribed. He and the people saved Agag, the robber king of Amalek, as well as the best of all the animals, refusing to "utterly destroy" them. Saul chose what seemed to him to be good, over what God had decreed through Samuel. And once again he refused to take responsibility for his sin, at first pretending to have followed God's instructions, then blaming the people.

Thus he fell into the same trap used by the devil in the Garden of Eden, convincing Eve that the forbidden fruit was good, rather than cleaving to the clear directive of God. Eve had decided for herself to eat of the Tree of Knowledge of Good and Evil. Now Saul decided for himself to hang on to what seemed good, rather than obey God.

It is a common trap still used by the enemy today. We may feel we know better. But if we go our own way rather than God's, we will forfeit our prophetic purpose, and the robber will have succeeded in keeping us out of our destiny.

Although Samuel, in the face of Saul's disobedience, took matters into his own hands and killed Agag, king of Amalek, somehow Agag's lineage remained. Hundreds of years later, in the book of Esther, we find Haman, who identified as an Agagite, a descendant of Agag, attempting the genocide of the

130

Jewish people in Persia. In Haman's mind it probably represented payback for how Israel tried to wipe out his entire tribe.

We will deal thoroughly with Haman and his ten sons in a later chapter. But history begs the question of what would have happened had Saul fully obeyed God.

If we do not fully obey what God has instructed, it may come back to haunt us or future generations.

Once again, the heart of the matter was not just Saul's disobedience, but his response when confronted with his sin. Saul proudly announced to Samuel, "I have performed the commandment of the LORD" (1 Samuel 15:13).

Samuel responded, "What then is this bleating of the sheep . . . and the lowing of the oxen?" (verse 14).

Immediately Saul blamed the people, saying, in effect: "The people made the decision to save these animals so they could offer them to your God" (see verse 15). In other words, "It's not my fault, it's *your* God and the fault of these people."

God had already told Samuel He was sorry He had made Saul king. Saul had not only disobeyed God's plan but erected a monument to himself, celebrating his own greatness. So Samuel challenged Saul again with the word of the Lord, restating that God had chosen Saul to be leader of His people and sent him on God's mission to utterly destroy His sworn enemy. Samuel asked, "Why then did you not obey the voice of the LORD? Why did you swoop down on the spoil, and do evil in the sight of the LORD?" (verse 19).

Saul's response shows just how blinded by pride he was. His very words condemned him:

> But I have obeyed the voice of the LORD, and gone on the mission on which the LORD sent me, and brought back Agag king of Amalek; I have utterly destroyed the Amalekites. But the people took of the plunder, sheep and oxen, the best of the

things which should have been utterly destroyed, to sacrifice to the LORD your God in Gilgal.

verses 20–21

Samuel responded with these words:

Has the LORD as great delight in burnt offerings and sacrifices, as in obeying the voice of the LORD? Behold, to obey is better than sacrifice, and to heed than the fat of rams. For rebellion is as the sin of witchcraft, and stubbornness is as iniquity and idolatry. Because you have rejected the word of the LORD, He also has rejected you from being king. . . . The LORD has torn the kingdom of Israel from you today, and has given it to a neighbor of yours, who is better than you.

verses 22–23, 28

From that day forward Samuel never visited Saul again, and a distressing spirit came upon Saul. He never again experienced God's blessings.

God of the Second Chance

Can a believer miss out on his or her destiny? Can prophecies fail? Can the word of the Lord not come to pass? Sad to say, the answer is yes.

Having been in prophetic ministry for more than forty years, I have heard mighty prophetic promises given over individuals' lives, only to see them go their own way, deceived into thinking God would overlook their sin and continue with His purpose to use and bless them. They can blame the devil, other people, circumstances, even God Himself. But ultimately it is their own pride and self-will that have derailed their destiny.

I know the story of Saul's downfall seems a bit depressing and hopeless, but the good news is that we are operating under grace and serving the God of the second chance—and often the third and fourth chance as well.

God gave Peter a second chance, even after he denied the Lord in His hour of need. Peter repented and recovered his prophetic purpose, leading thousands to Christ and pioneering the New Testament Church. God chose a fearful failure and turned him into a powerful preacher.

Another young man, "John, also called Mark" (Acts 12:25 NIV), joined Paul on his first missionary journey. But the way was hard and seemed to bear little fruit, so John Mark, perhaps discouraged, abandoned Paul and quit the mission. Later Barnabas and Paul argued about giving John Mark another chance, and their dispute actually caused them to part ways. Paul refused to take the "quitter" along and launched out on his second missionary journey with Silas instead; while Barnabas (whose name means "son of encouragement," see Acts 4:36) took John Mark on a mission of his own. (Read the story in Acts 15:36–41.) Barnabas gave John Mark a second chance.

Years later Paul called John Mark a fellow worker in the Gospel; and while he was in prison in Rome, he actually called for John Mark to be sent to him "because he is helpful to me in my ministry" (2 Timothy 4:11 NIV; see also Colossians 4:10).

Bible scholars believe that this man, John (his Hebrew name), also called Mark (his Roman name), was the author of the gospel of Mark, basing this book on the eyewitness account of Peter.[2]

Our God is the God of the second chance, if we do not quit!

God of the Comeback

One of the definitions for *recovery* is "comeback." God once spoke to me and said to tell the people, "Your setbacks are merely setups for a mighty comeback." Although I heard this from the Lord, I have since realized that many have used this phrase. I believe God is emphasizing to His Church that He is indeed the God of the comeback.

The word *comeback* is defined as "a return to formerly enjoyed status or prosperity; a return to popularity";[3] or "a return to a former good position or condition; a new effort to win or succeed after being close to defeat or failure."[4]

Comeback Stories

The Bible is full of comeback stories in which it seems all hope of fulfillment is lost, but God stages a mighty comeback for His people. Here are just a few:

- Moses was a murderer and a fugitive who became a deliverer, known as a prophet and friend of God.
- Joseph was a dreamer, sold into slavery, forgotten in prison in a foreign land, who became the prime minister of the greatest empire of the day.
- David was an adulterer and murderer who became the greatest king Israel ever knew, whose legacy is also that he was a man after God's own heart.
- Job lost everything through no fault of his own, yet God restored double for what he lost.
- The Temple was destroyed but then rebuilt, with Persian money.
- Peter denied Christ three times but was used by God to preach to and win three thousand souls on the Day of Pentecost.
- Jesus—in the greatest comeback story of them all—was beaten, crucified, killed, and placed in a tomb, yet He conquered death, hell, and the grave by coming back to life, and is now seated with honor at the right hand of God!

An Army Rising Up

One of the greatest pictures of a comeback is the image of the valley of dry bones in Ezekiel 37. God took the prophet out to a valley that had dry bones scattered all over the ground. It was a picture of an army that had suffered a tremendous defeat, and in an act of ultimate dishonor, the bones of the dead were left to rot and dry in the desert sun. It was the picture of utter devastation, hopelessness, and failure.

The phrase *dry bones* comes from the Hebrew word *yabesh*, which is the convergence of three words—*shame, confusion*, and *disappointment*,[5] which causes things to dry up and wither away.

God said to the prophet, "Can these bones live?" and the prophet responded, "O Lord GOD, You know." What he may have been saying is, "I really don't think so, but obviously You see something different."

You may feel as if your prophetic purpose resembles the valley of dry bones. You have walked through deep disappointment, confusion, and disillusionment, and all the shame that comes with it. You may even believe you have lost your chance at seeing your destiny fulfilled. But look what happened to those dry bones. God told the prophet to prophesy to them, saying, "O dry bones, hear the word of the LORD!" (verse 4). The word of the Lord brings life. Prophesy life into that which is dead.

Ezekiel did as God commanded and the dry bones responded. The prophecy caused a shaking, and suddenly what was dead came back to life. The bones began to come together, and then flesh came upon them. But there was still no breath in them.

Then God instructed Ezekiel to prophesy life and breath from the four winds, so he did. The word *breath* is the Hebrew word *ruach*, which means wind, breath, life,[6] referring to the

Spirit of God; and also "an inspiring ecstatic state of prophecy that utters instruction or warning, imparting warlike energy and executive and administrative power, a manifestation of the shekinah glory of God."[7] (*Shekinah* is the English transliteration of a Hebrew word that appears in the Talmud and refers to the manifestation of the presence or glory of God.) This is what happens when we prophesy; we call dead things to life! The dry bones, which were previously dead, lived and stood on their feet, "an exceedingly great army" (verse 10).

During the pandemic Tom and I prayed and prophesied to a woman who had been on a ventilator for eleven days. The doctors said she was failing and there was nothing more they could do. But the Lord told us to prophesy the *ruach* (breath) of God into her lungs, just as in Ezekiel's picture. Within the hour, her oxygen jumped from the low sixties to the high nineties. And within a day and a half, she was off the ventilator and completely healed and restored.

A PROPHETIC WORD FOR YOU

The Lord says: *There is an army rising up, full of warlike energy, courage, and the glory of God. Those who have felt discouraged and defeated, hopeless in pursuit of their promise, are being infused with My resurrection life. If you feel you have lost your way, I charge you now to believe that a comeback is possible. Don't give up! Shake off despair. Hear the word of the Lord. Read your Bible and listen to your prophetic promises. Decree them with your mouth. Know that your time has come. Receive My breath into your body, soul, and spirit, and rise to fulfill your prophetic purpose. I am anointing you to move with the spirit of Ezekiel upon you, calling dead things to life.*

A DECREE TO TAKE BACK YOUR PURPOSE

[Speak this aloud in faith!] *I will arise and fulfill my prophetic purpose. I will obey Your voice, Lord, and answer Your call. I repent for the times I have, like Saul, rebelled against You and failed to obey Your voice. Deliver me from any curse resulting from my own bad choices. I will pursue You with my whole heart. Though I may suffer some setbacks, they will only be setups for a mighty comeback in my life. Be the God of my comeback. The thief will not succeed in keeping me from fulfilling the call of God on my life. I submit myself totally to You and ask You to breathe Your* ruach *breath inside of me, filling me with power and manifesting the* shekinah *glory of God in and through my life. In Jesus' name I declare this.*

QUESTIONS TO CONSIDER

1. Can you identify choices you have made that may have placed a limitation on your expectation to fulfill your destiny? If so, take time to pray prayers of repentance. David's prayer of repentance in Psalm 51 is a good example. When he had sinned and placed his legacy in jeopardy, David humbled himself and got back on track with his calling.

2. Is there an area in which you feel you have suffered a setback and have not yet seen the comeback? If so, be bold enough to write a decree over that area, declaring God's divine purpose for a comeback.

3. Can you identify an area in your life that may be like the valley of dry bones, filled with shame, confusion, or disappointment? If so, prophesy to those dry bones and say, "Hear the word of the Lord."

SEVEN

TAKING BACK OUR POSTERITY

Pursue . . . overtake them and without fail recover all.

1 Samuel 30:8

Have you ever had to confront the thief for your marriage, your children, or your grandchildren? Have you ever had to engage in battle for the salvation and destinies of family members? Have you ever had to pray for a prodigal son or daughter to return to the Lord? Have you engaged in praying for your city or the nation in which you are called to live? A big part of our calling in Christ is contending for nations and generations. To accomplish this, we must establish Kingdom dominion through building strong families and creating generational synergy, thereby bringing societal change.

In her recent book *Fire on the Family Altar*, Cheryl Sacks relates something the Lord spoke to her regarding families. She says she was getting ready to step onto a platform to lead a large group in prayer for the nation, when God said to her, *Revival will come to America when the family altar is restored.*[1]

The family altar has to do with family prayer, reading God's Word together, telling the stories of all God has done in the past, and creating an environment in the home for God's presence and power to dwell. When we create a place for the Lord, not just in our churches but in our homes, revival fires are stirred to change nations and generations. When our children are taught to love Jesus, they are empowered as they grow to maturity to confront the thief.

The Battle Is Real

One of the greatest personal battles my husband and I have fought is over the lives and destinies of our children and grandchildren. As a young mother, I suffered the heartbreak of multiple miscarriages. But we were blessed with two beautiful daughters and our amazing son.

When I was pregnant with our first daughter, the doctor said she was in my fallopian tube and would have to be removed— meaning aborted. He told us that if we did not do this, my tube would burst and not only would I lose the baby, but it could kill me. Tom and I resisted and asked for a week to pray about this. The doctor was not happy about this decision.

A week later, when we returned to tell him we had decided to continue the pregnancy, he examined me again and said, amazed, that the fetus had "somehow" moved into the womb, which he said "doesn't happen." Our daughter's life was saved, and she is a beautiful woman today.

Our son was born with a severe facial birth defect that required thirteen reconstructive surgeries to repair. God gave Tom and Jason and me grace to face each challenge. Jason is now a handsome man with a beautiful wife and three boys of his own.

One of my grandsons, while still in the womb, was diagnosed with a hole in his heart, which was completely healed by his time of birth, as a result of our praying and decreeing healing and life over him. Another grandson was born with a genetic condition called Williams syndrome. If you have heard me preach or read any of my other books, you have probably run across some of the stories of miracles for our special boy Lucas. God gave us prophetic words at key times in his life that produced healing and miracles in his heart, brain, and leg, and in the process of his growth and development.

As I embarked on writing this book, our family was challenged yet again. We went on a Christmas vacation because most of my grandkids had never seen snow. As we were traveling by plane, our twelve-year-old granddaughter suffered from a series of "absence seizures." By the time our plane landed, she did not recognize her parents and was so confused she thought she was only five years old. Paramedics had to come and evacuate her from the plane into an ambulance, taking her to a local children's hospital. After a few days she was released and seemed fine.

A week later, as we boarded our flight to return home, our daughter Tiffany suffered from a tonic-clonic seizure (previously known as a grand mal seizure), which had never happened before. It seemed bizarre in light of what had occurred just a week before with her daughter. During her seizure Tiffany stopped breathing, and it seemed as if the life went out of her. We all prayed and decreed life to come back into her. Her nine-year-old son cried out, "Jesus, I know You're a God who does miracles. Do a miracle for my mom, in Jesus' name!" Suddenly Tiffany began to breathe again. She, too, was evacuated medically from the plane and taken immediately to an area hospital. Such an attack—but oh, the faithfulness of God!

A year later, at the time of this writing, Tiffany and her daughter are both doing well and are full of faith. Although some things have been diagnosed in each of them, they continue to believe for a full manifestation of God's healing in their lives. But it has been quite the battle.

God has been faithful to us through many challenges and physical difficulties. But it has been a battle against an enemy who seeks to afflict our family and our generations, trying to cut off their destinies and even their lives.

Generational Dominion

Why is there so much spiritual warfare regarding families? When God placed man and woman in the Garden, He gave them a mandate to "be fruitful and multiply [have kids]; fill the earth and subdue it; have dominion" (Genesis 1:28). Our God-given assignment to rule the earth could be accomplished only through generational dominion, passing the principles of the Kingdom generationally.

One of the ways the thief wants to rob us is through generational disruption, taking our legacy and cutting off our posterity—future or succeeding generations,[2] those coming after us. Posterity includes those in our bloodline (children and grandchildren), as well as those we have mentored, discipled, and imparted to—our spiritual heritage and legacy.

The robber is after our natural and our spiritual kids. He wants to afflict natural and spiritual families. Why? Because the enemy hates generational continuity, knowing that strong families produce the rule of the Kingdom of God in the earth. Kingdom dominion in the earth happens when generations connect synergistically—meaning we are all stronger together.

It is the very nature of God to connect generations. He identifies Himself as the God of Abraham, Isaac, and Jacob. He is a multigenerational God.

We see this modeled in 2 Timothy 1:5, when Paul is exhorting his spiritual son Timothy. He says he "[calls] to remembrance the genuine faith that is in you, which dwelt first in your grandmother Lois and your mother Eunice, and I am persuaded is in you also." Generations were designed to work together to produce the living principles of the Kingdom, laying a foundation for future success.

In my family and church, four generations are worshiping and working together for the glory of God. Tom's dad, Bishop Bill Hamon, is the founder of our ministry, Christian International. Tom's brother, Tim, his sister, Sherilyn, and I co-labor in running the church and ministry. Now our daughter Tiffany and her husband, Jason, are functioning in pastoral leadership roles. Their daughter serves on the worship team with a heart and passion to pursue Jesus.

This, I believe, is what a family and ministry should look like. But the devil hates it! In fact, he is terrified of the power and dominion produced when generations work together.

The devil has been strategically targeting the generations, particularly over the last several decades, in an attempt not only to destroy families but to fray the fabric of society and steal the destiny of nations.

The 1960s saw the hippie and free love movement. In 1967 college-age students massed in the Haight-Ashbury neighborhood of San Francisco in what was called the "Summer of Love"—which was actually the summer of rebellion. In the 1970s high school students got caught up in the sex, drug, and rock-and-roll culture. The 1980s and '90s saw an increase in drug and alcohol use among pre-teens. Now we see elementary and even pre-kindergarten children as the targets of the homosexual and transgender ideologies and agendas.

It is the enemy's goal to create a prodigal generation that has forgotten God and sees no place for Him in their lives. But

God is calling prodigals home, back to His heart, back to His Kingdom. We must contend for the spiritual lives of our children and grandchildren. Our future depends on it.

If we lose generations, we will lose nations. It was for this reason that God instructed Israel to continuously teach the truths of God to their children and grandchildren (see Deuteronomy 4:9; 11:19). When Israel forgot to teach her children the ways of God, another generation arose who did not know the Lord or His ways. As a result, the nation became subject to being plundered and taken into captivity (see Judges 2:10–19).

Our children are the leaders of our future. Without a biblical worldview regarding the Lord and His ways, enabling the next generation to shape policies, laws, and agendas, leaders will falter and nations will be affected. We must have generational continuity of spiritual principles, taught and then applied to public life, in order to hold the line against the advancement of evil in the land.

The Curse of Fatherlessness

God identifies Himself not only as a multigenerational God, but as a Father. Jesus taught us to pray to our heavenly Father, and He introduced us to the Father's loving heart. Second Corinthians 6:18 says, quoting the Old Testament, "I will be a Father to you, and you shall be My sons and daughters, says the LORD Almighty." God is the Creator of families, and He models this in our spiritual relationship with Him.

But the world is in crisis, rooted in rebellion against God and the subsequent curse of fatherlessness, which is destroying generations and robbing families of stability and security.

Malachi 4:6 says this about the prophetic spirit of Elijah: "He will turn the hearts of the fathers to the children, and the hearts of the children to their fathers, lest I come and strike the earth with a curse." Generational disconnection brings a curse in the land that leads to destruction, not just of families but of nations.

Statistics indicate that homes without fathers produce all manner of instability in children. According to Edward Kruk, a Canadian sociologist and social worker:

> 71% of high school dropouts are fatherless; fatherless children have more trouble academically, scoring poorly on tests of reading, mathematics, and thinking skills; children from father-absent homes are more likely to play truant from school, more likely to be excluded from school, more likely to leave school at age 16, and less likely to attain academic and professional qualifications in adulthood.[3]

According to the National Fatherhood Initiative, which examines data from the U.S. Census Bureau, children in father-absent homes are four times more likely to be poor, and are more likely to have behavioral problems, commit crime, drop out of school, abuse alcohol, deal drugs, and go to prison.[4] It is clear that growing up in a two-parent home matters to the health, well-being, and future of the next generation.

If you are a single parent, this is not meant to produce guilt or shame. There are many valid reasons individuals may find themselves parenting alone. We celebrate women who choose life rather than abortion. We recognize that continuing infidelity by a partner presents a valid biblical reason for divorce. And no one wants to see someone living in a physically abusive relationship. But in Malachi 2:16 the Lord declares that He hates divorce. The New English Translation renders the last part of this verse "Pay attention to your conscience, and do not be unfaithful."

It is important to recognize that on a societal level, God intended for there to be two loving parents in a home—a father and a mother. When this structure breaks down, there may be consequences for the next generation. This makes it even more important for us to fight for healthy, godly marriages and strong, stable, God-fearing families, in order to see the societal curse reversed.

The Peril of Disconnection

Winston Churchill, prime minister of the United Kingdom, in part during the most challenging years of World War II, advocated fighting for our generations:

> One of the signs of a great society is the diligence with which it passes culture from one generation to the next. This culture is the embodiment of everything the people of that society hold dear: its religious faith, its heroes. When one generation no longer esteems its own heritage and fails to pass the torch to its children, it is saying in essence that the very foundational principles and experiences that make the society what it is are no longer valid. This leaves that generation without any sense of definition or direction, making them the fulfillment of Karl Marx's dictum, "A people without a heritage are easily persuaded." What is required when this happens, and the society has lost its way, is for leaders to arise who have not forgotten the discarded legacy and who love it with all their hearts. They can then become the voice of that lost generation, wooing an errant generation back to the faith of their fathers, back to the ancient foundations and the bedrock values.[5]

We see the peril of generational disconnection in the Old Testament story of Gideon, who defeated the Midianite and Amalekite robbers. He won mighty victories in his generation. But he failed as a father because he did not teach his sons to fight.

145

The Old Testament warrior Gideon captured Zebah and Zalmunna, two kings of Midian, and he told his son Jether to kill them. "But the youth would not draw his sword; for he was afraid, because he was still a youth" (Judges 8:20). So Gideon took his own sword and killed them instead.

Gideon was a mighty warrior, used powerfully by God, but he failed to teach his own sons to fight. The description of Jether as a youth meant that he was a teenager. In ancient times children and youth were trained at an early age to fight. And by setting before Jether two kings who were already bound and defeated, Gideon had the perfect opportunity to help his son gain a reputation as one who killed enemy kings. But Jether would not do his father's bidding because he was afraid. This exposes a lack of training by Gideon in preparing his sons for battle.

In Judges 9 we see the tragic result. Abimelech, the son of Gideon's concubine, rose up and in one day killed seventy of Gideon's sons. Had they been trained for battle more effectively, this probably would not have occurred and Gideon's legacy would have been preserved.

Fathers and mothers, it is important that we pass our spiritual inheritance on to succeeding generations, and show them how to fight for their legacy as well. The reason? Generational disconnection is taking place throughout the earth fueled by a spiritual thief called the orphan spirit.

An orphan is a child whose parents have died, or even a person who has been abandoned physically or emotionally by living parents. My dear friend Dr. Sandie Freed has written extensively about this demonic attack in her book *Warfare Strategies for Kingdom Advancement*. Dr. Sandie writes:

When an individual is deprived of a parent's love and care, a false belief gradually takes root that constantly whispers: "I am unlovable; I am ashamed; I'm abandoned; I must perform to be loved." The orphan believes God loves others, just not him/her. Therefore, an orphan's self-esteem, self-respect, self-assurance, and so forth is affected, until he or she gets free from an orphan mindset and an orphan spirit.[6]

A generation today is suffering under an orphan spirit. The lies of the enemy have created a generation gap, leaving them lonely, frustrated, and often in despair. It takes strong, healthy spiritual mothers and fathers to fight for families, heal their wounds, and woo the lost generation back to God.

Generational Robbery at Ziklag

Before David became king, he and his six hundred men were hiding from King Saul in the Philistine town of Ziklag, when we find the thieves, the Amalekites, at it again. While David and his men were away at a battle, the Amalekites swooped down on the encampment and stole not only their possessions but all their family members—wives and children. "Then David and the people who were with him lifted up their voices and wept, until they had no more power to weep" (1 Samuel 30:4).

When the enemy comes after our marriages and families, it is one of the most heartbreaking, soul-aching battles you will fight. David's mighty warriors were so broken they cried until they had no tears left. They even thought of stoning David to take their grief out on him.

Hearing God in Crisis

David's response to his own grief and the distress of his men was, first, to "[strengthen] himself in the LORD his God" (verse 6). His next response was to inquire of the Lord.

When we find ourselves in times of distress, we must learn to do the same. Too often we run to every other possible solution for our problem—even good things such as counselors, prayer partners, or pastors. Or we may seek the comfort of unproductive things to numb our senses in a time of crisis—things such as entertainment, food, alcohol, or other distractions—rather than listen to God. May each of us seek to become more and more like David in our response to crisis.

David came to the Lord with his problems and questions. Now again, rather than give in to anger, fear, self-pity, or hopelessness, he sought the voice of the Lord.

> David inquired of the LORD, saying, "Shall I pursue this troop? Shall I overtake them?" And He answered him, "Pursue, for you shall surely overtake them and without fail recover all."
>
> 1 Samuel 30:8

So David and his men went after the Amalekites, located and attacked them, and "recovered all that the Amalekites had carried away" (verse 18).

Pursue, Overtake, and Recover All

I have found at critical moments that the Lord is a very present help in time of need. He desires to meet with us, to comfort us, and to communicate with us. His presence is tangible, if only we will still ourselves to hear Him.

After our daughter and granddaughter were diagnosed with some medical issues after their seizures, I sought the Lord. That night I had a dream in which the Lord spoke to me and said to tell the family, *I am not asking you to deny the reality of the diagnosis, but I am asking you to deny its authority over your life.* In other words, some natural things may need to be dealt with until the manifestation of full healing, but they should not allow the diagnosis to take a position of authority over their lives.

In times of crisis, God is always able to give us a word that we can use to contend with the enemy. The voice of the Lord shatters the enemy (see Isaiah 30:31 NIV)! God's assurance to David at Ziklag should become the decree for every believer who has been victimized by the spirit of robbery: "Pursue, overtake, and recover all!"

So if the enemy has robbed your children or grandchildren of the promise of abundant life: Pursue, overtake, and recover all!

If the enemy has drawn your family members away from a relationship with the Lord and caused them to fall into prodigal status: Pursue, overtake, and recover all!

If your family has suffered needless grief from trauma, sickness, or loss: Pursue, overtake, and recover all!

If the spirit of robbery has caused distress, hopelessness, and grief: Pursue, overtake, and recover all!

God's promise regarding our families is this: "Thus says the LORD: . . . I will contend with him who contends with you, and I will save your children" (Isaiah 49:25).

The Power of Connection

In chapter 4 we talked about the effects of generational curses. More needs to be written, however, about generational blessings. These are the positive influences, breakthroughs, and gifts that come by being generationally connected. In fact, experiencing healthy generational relationships can be one of the most powerful gifts a person can receive.

When children enjoy the blessing of being raised by two God-fearing, healthy parents, it sets them up for all kinds of advantages in life. The National Center for Fathering says,

> Children with involved, loving fathers are significantly more likely to do well in school, have healthy self-esteem, exhibit

empathy and pro-social behavior, and avoid high-risk behaviors such as drug use, truancy, and criminal activity compared to children who have uninvolved fathers.

Studies on parent-child relationships and child wellbeing show that a father's love is an important factor in predicting the social, emotional, and cognitive development and functioning of children and young adults.[7]

Perhaps you were not afforded this opportunity in your natural family. But you can connect to the heart of our heavenly Father to find love and healing. Additionally, the Kingdom of God gives you the opportunity to forge new relationships with spiritual fathers and mothers who can mentor you, help you grow, and become a success. Local churches become vital in forming communities in which children raised in single-parent households can be healed and supported.

Tom and I were blessed to be raised by all four of our biological parents. Besides that, I had spiritual parents early in my Christian walk. Then, later, Tom's parents, Bill and Evelyn Hamon, became my spiritual parents, with whom we have worked in ministry our entire marriage. Although some might say that working with family can be a challenge, we have found it one of our greatest blessings.

So Tom and I have been the recipients of generational blessings from our parents, which set us up to become effective spiritual parents for others. We have pastored for close to forty years and have seen those from broken, dysfunctional natural families find a home in the family of God in our local church. They have been able to receive from the power of connection and have gone on to have families of their own, with great success.

The cycle in the Kingdom of God is for each of us to find our place in the family of God. Each believer, once having received the blessing of being fathered or mothered spiritually, should in turn grow up in Christ to become a spiritual father or mother. The apostle Paul had no problem calling Timothy his son. This was a spiritual positioning, not a biological one. As fathers and mothers, each of us should receive the challenge of finding others to pour ourselves into—investing in them, discipling them, coaching them, mentoring them.

Call for Spiritual Fathers and Mothers

Spiritual fathers and mothers provide at least seven traits that help lay a success track in life and ministry for succeeding generations.

1. Courage

It takes tremendous courage to follow Jesus and do what He says. It takes courage to answer God's call. As a matter of fact, if you are going to live a life of obedience to Christ, you can be assured He is going to ask things of you that will challenge you out of your comfort zone. Truthfully, some of what He asks of you may scare you out of your mind!

When you determine to walk out the destiny God has called you to, the enemy will come and attempt to rob you of your courage and put you in fear. The word *discourage* basically means to take away someone's courage so he or she will lose heart.[8] The enemy will use fear, intimidation, uncertainty, and other negative emotions to attempt to keep you from pursuing what God has called you to.

I have always been an extrovert. I am outgoing, have never met a stranger, and do not suffer from stage fright. But, as I mentioned earlier, I faced a constant internal battle in my younger years with fear.

I was thirty years old and afraid of the dark. I was afraid of snakes. I was, honestly, afraid of the devil and his power. I was afraid of failing or not measuring up to others' expectations. I was afraid of not being a good enough mother. I was afraid of not fully fulfilling God's call on my life. I struggled with vain imaginations and fear of early death. I felt ashamed and inauthentic because I could be bold in public but was still rocked by personal, private fears. I truly understood what 1 John 4:18 means when it says that "fear involves torment."

One day our staff was doing an exercise in which we shared the value we received from the other members of our team. When it was my turn, person after person commented on how I inspired them with courage. This really surprised me, and I commented on how I constantly battled fear and certainly did not feel brave. Then my brother-in-law, Tim Hamon, told me that I did not understand the concept of courage. Courage, he said, was not the absence of fear, but the ability to face fear and overcome it.

I realized that day that I could be both fearful and brave. Courage gave me the ability to confront and overcome my fears.

When you feel hindered by fears and insecurities, this is where spiritual fathers and mothers come in. They have the power to encourage you when you feel discouraged. To encourage means to put courage into you. The root word in Latin is *cour*, the word for heart.[9] When parents put courage in you, they give you the ability to live life with your whole heart, undiminished by fears and doubts. They do this through encouraging words, and also the examples of their own successes and even failures.

Tom's and my spiritual parents gave us courage to raise a good family in the midst of ministry, to lead a congregation, to respond in faith during times of personal crisis or financial lack, to travel to the nations, and even to speak and minister to national leaders, all because they paved the way with their own life experiences. They made it seem more natural and less daunting. They did it, so we felt we could do it, too.

2. Dreaming Big Dreams

My mother grew up in an age when many career opportunities were not afforded to women. When I was a child, she would tell me, "Jane, don't ever let someone tell you you can't do something or be something because you were born a woman." I was always a go-getter. I had three brothers and believed I was as tough as they were in any given situation. When I met Jesus and heard Him call me into ministry, I began to dream big dreams about my life and destiny.

But in my early years of being a woman in ministry, I faced prejudices and limitations within the organized Church. My mother's words rang in my heart and gave me courage to be who God had called me to be.

My father has always been up for an adventure. I believe he gave me the spirit of adventure and love of travel, which helped shape me for my dream of touching the world. Tom and I have a passion to see the world. We hope this is something we have imparted to our natural children as well as to our spiritual kids.

Likewise, Tom's parents encouraged me constantly to step up and be who God called me to be. When I felt shaken by criticism, Bishop put courage in me to be bold and strong.

Once, while I was dealing with some negative things that had been spoken about me, Bishop said, "Jane, there will always be lots of voices and opinions about you. Some will love you, others will criticize. You need to learn to choose the voices you give weight to. Tom, Mom, and I will always tell you the truth about yourself. If you let our voices be the most important voices in your life, you can be as bold as you dare to be, and if you are not doing something right, we will tell you. This way the voice of your critics won't have power over you."

This gave me courage in the face of criticism to dream big dreams and be all God called me to be.

3. The Impartation of Wisdom

Deuteronomy 34:9 says, "Joshua the son of Nun was full of the spirit of wisdom, for Moses had laid his hands on him; so the children of Israel heeded him, and did as the LORD had commanded Moses." Joshua both learned wisdom and was imparted wisdom by Moses. Moses had learned wisdom through years of trial and error. He met face to face with God and was touched by His glory. This gave him something to impart to Joshua, which enabled the younger man to become the great leader who conquered the Promised Land.

The next generation (represented by Joshua) needs to look for leaders who have seen the Lord and been empowered by the Holy Spirit (represented by Moses). It is through these personal encounters with God that those leaders, spiritual mothers and fathers, have something real to impart to the next generation.

Mordecai imparted wisdom and strategy to Esther, telling her not to reveal her heritage as a Jew to anyone until it was time. She gleaned from Mordecai's wisdom and experience and did not have to figure everything else out by herself. What a blessing to have others who can lead and guide through wisdom, so the next generation does not have to figure everything out for themselves.

Paul told the Romans, "I long to see you, that I may impart to you some spiritual gift, so that you may be established" (Romans 1:11). There is power in laying hands on someone and imparting something to that person for free that you have suffered and paid a price for. The laying on of hands, remember, is one of the "elementary principles of Christ" (Hebrews 6:1–2). So never underestimate the power of impartation—from one person to the next, from one generation to the next.

I have had several important times of impartation in my life. I received the laying on of hands and impartation from Bishop

Hamon, who released boldness and accuracy in the prophetic. He laid hands on me and activated the gift of discernment in my life, which caused a veil to be removed so I could see more clearly in the spirit realm. Everything changed for me that day (which I write about in detail in my book *Discernment: The Essential Guide to Hearing the Voice of God*).

I also received an impartation for boldness as a woman in ministry from Dr. Fuchsia Pickett, an older spiritual mother who pioneered in the area of being a strong woman in ministry. Something happened inside me when she laid hands on me and prayed, releasing a mantle of prophetic teaching and boldness on my life. (I write about much of my journey as a woman in ministry in my book *The Deborah Company*.)

I also received the laying on of hands from a psalmist who activated in me the ability to write songs. I do not think of myself as a songwriter since I do not play any musical instruments. But since that time, I have actually written or helped write a few songs, some which have been recorded.

Something miraculous happens when we lay hands on others and impart things to them for which we had to fight or even pioneer. On the other hand, it is equally amazing when we receive things from an impartation and have them activated in our lives, things that were absent or dormant before.

It is not possible to release an impartation for every area of life, as there are things individuals must go through in their own growing process in Christ. But when possible, it is a tremendous blessing and joy to freely give the next generation of leaders an advantage.

4. A Sense of Identity

Parents are given the responsibility to name their children. A child's name matters, as it distinguishes him or her as a unique individual.

In Scripture great significance is attached to names. In the Old Testament, names identified aspects of expected calling, characteristics, and capacities. Names even marked the history of a nation. Abram, whose name meant *father*, was changed to Abraham, which means *father of nations*. Jacob, whose name meant *supplanter* or *deceiver*, was changed to Israel, meaning *prince with God* or *he who struggles with God*.

Identity comes from more than what a parent has named a child; it comes from the vision, expectation, and identity spoken over that child on a daily basis. As both natural and spiritual parents, we need to examine if we are speaking limitless dreams or limited experience. Are we declaring possibilities or telling our children what they cannot do? Are we fueling their faith or feeding their fears?

Strong identity will bring a child security; and insecurity will breed immaturity. Proverbs 23:7 declares that as a person "thinks in his heart, so is he." When two blind men asked Jesus to heal them, He responded, "According to your faith be it unto you" (Matthew 9:29 KJV). I love the way *The Message* puts it: "Become what you believe." This tells us that our internal belief about what we can and cannot do will determine our behavior and outcome. Our identity will either empower us to overcome, or sabotage and destroy us.

How important is it for parents, then, to fill our children's hearts and minds with a God-centered identity?

AN IDENTITY DECREE

[Speak this aloud in faith!] *I am made in the image of God. His DNA flows through my veins. I am created in His image, nature, character, and likeness; therefore, aspects of His nature dwell in me. If He is Elohim, the Creator, I have the power for creativity within me. If He is El Shaddai, God Almighty, I have*

His power, might, and ability within me. If He is Jehovah Jireh, the Lord my Provider, I have the seeds of wealth and provision within me. If He is Jehovah Rapha, the Lord my Healer, I have the power to do miracles and walk in health. If He is Jehovah Shalom, God of Peace, I have the ability to live in peace and security. If He is Jehovah Tsebaoth, the Lord of Hosts, the Lord of the Angel Armies, I have the seed of the warrior inside of me and can overcome all things.

IDENTITY SHIFT

When we get identity right, it removes limitations. One way or the other, children will live up to the reputation their parents project toward them. If they are called stupid, they will live under that limitation. If they are encouraged that they are smart, can learn, and can succeed in school, the sky is the limit.

My husband's mom, Evelyn Hamon, used to tell this story about Tom. When he was two, he was a big boy and a bit of a bully. He picked on his older brother, Tim, and other kids. They called him "Tommy the Terror" and "Tommy the Tank." One day Tom's parents got hold of a book that talked about giving your child the reputation you wanted him or her to live up to. So they changed their language and the identity they projected toward little Tommy. They began to say things like "Tommy's our good boy" and "Our good boy would never do things like that." Within a few days, Tommy had an attitude change. He wanted to be the good boy rather than the terror. His identity shift set him up to become a good man, full of kindness and integrity.

5. Covering

Natural and spiritual mothers and fathers provide a spiritual covering for their children. Paul told the Romans, "Day and night I bring you and your needs in prayer to God" (Romans

1:9 NLT), and again to the Thessalonians, "We continue to pray night and day most earnestly that we may see you face to face, and may complete whatever may be imperfect and lacking in your faith" (1 Thessalonians 3:10 AMP).

Spiritual parents must fight for the destiny and spiritual inheritance of the succeeding generation by praying for them and covering them from every demonic attack that tries to rob them. Moses' rod of authority served as a covering for Joshua and his sword when they went to battle against the Amalekites. Mordecai prayed for Esther when she went before the king, knowing her life was at stake. Paul prayed for his son Timothy when he was facing Nero's persecution of believers, telling him to "be strong in the Lord and in the power of His might" (Ephesians 6:10).

Parents may not be able to prevent the challenges and battles the next generation must face, but we can do our best to teach, train, and prepare them, praying for them all the way. Your prayers may not prevent the storms, but they can provide an umbrella to protect them in the midst of them. This breaks the assignments of isolation, independence, and loneliness that have plagued younger generations, letting them know they do not have to do life on their own.

6. Place and Permission

It is a joy for leaders and spiritual parents to see the next generation step into areas of boldness in the Holy Spirit in which we had to pioneer. In the early days of prophetic ministry, it took great boldness to hear a word from God and step up to the platform to speak a prophetic word to the congregation. Now, not only is my children's generation able to prophesy, but their children are following the example. It is not unusual in our church for a five- or six-year-old to step up to Tom or me during worship and say, "I have a word from God." As leaders, we give place and permission for them to share what is on their hearts.

My kids started going to the mission field in their early teens and saw people healed, even a blind eye opened, when they prayed. Today we see a whole generation of bold, prophetic healing evangelists arising.

In one service in our church, I sensed that the Holy Spirit wanted to move in healing. Rather than call our elders or prayer teams, I felt the Lord say to call up the children and have them lay hands on the sick. We had many testimonies that Sunday, from people both present and online, of healings they received when the children prayed.

It is time we join the generations, giving place and position for the younger ones to step into their gifts and callings in Christ. I like to say that when our children are filled with the Spirit, they do not receive a junior Holy Spirit, but the same One we have been given, to move in power and miracles.

7. Generational Wealth

Proverbs 13:22 tells us, "A good man leaves an inheritance to his children's children." Wealth was meant to be passed generationally within the family. Again, if the enemy can cut off the family, he can cut off generational continuity in wealth.

In his book *Doing Business God's Way*, Dennis Peacocke devotes an entire chapter to this important subject in the context of creating Kingdom wealth and managing it for growth and productivity. He writes:

> God's blessing pipeline is the family unit: that is why the warfare around our families is so severe. If you weaken or destroy the family, you cut the pipeline of wealth and usually the next generation starts in the hole, not even.

He goes on to say:

> Our children are a stewardship, a heritage, an inheritance from the Lord. God requires us to pass on our wealth to them and to raise them in the faith as we teach them the truths and moral wealth-creating principles of scripture. . . . Lasting wealth is multi-generational. . . . The mistake many rich people make is never to teach their children to be wealthy.[10]

Clearly we need to stop thinking in terms of a single generation and begin to employ strategies for generational synergy in every area of life.

A Prophetic Word for You

The Lord says: *You have been engaged in the battle for your families, just as David had to rise up and battle the robbers for his. So I say to you what I said to him all those years ago: Pursue, overtake, and recover all! I am the Lord, who will fight along with you to see your family healed, delivered, preserved, and launched into their destiny and calling. Fight for your prodigals. Bring them into My heavenly court and receive My decrees over their lives. Bring them before My throne of grace and watch Me turn things around. Do not become grieved, disheartened, and give up. No matter your age, no matter their age, no matter what has gone on in the past, allow Me to release My help in your time of need. Nations are hanging in the balance. Rise up and fight for your generations and see Me also shift your nation.*

A DECREE TO TAKE BACK YOUR POSTERITY

[Speak this aloud in faith!] *I will arise as a spiritual parent and contend for the next generation. I will invest in them, pour into them, and pray for them. I break every assignment of the orphan spirit off my life and off the lives of my natural and spiritual children. I decree generational dominion, synergy, and continuity that will turn the curse to a blessing. In Jesus' name.*

QUESTIONS TO CONSIDER

1. What are some of the generational blessings you have received from your natural parents? What about your spiritual parents?

2. Do you recognize any traits of the orphan spirit being manifested in your life? If so, ask the Lord for freedom from wrong mindsets and deliverance from any demonic stronghold.

3. What are some ways you can invest in the next generation? What do you have to impart? How can you serve them?

EIGHT

TAKING BACK OUR HEALTH

They will lay hands on the sick, and they will recover.

Mark 16:18

One of the greatest battles believers fight is the one to appropriate the healing and miracle power of Jesus Christ in taking back health. At some point in your life, you will need to contend for healing for yourself or a loved one.

One of the things Christ commissioned His disciples to do before He ascended to heaven was to "lay hands on the sick," with the result that "they will recover" (Mark 16:18). We have been empowered to confront the thief of our health and take back abundant life.

In Deuteronomy 25:17–18, God reminded the Israelites that when they were coming out of Egypt, the Amalekites had attacked them from behind, taking out the "feeble" and the "faint and weary" (KJV). The word *feeble* is defined as weak, easily broken, frail.[1] The enemy loves to attack us physically, taking our strength, health, and vitality. God wants to restore it all, regardless of age, until our appointed time to go to heaven.

In Luke 4:16–19, when Jesus read from the scroll of Isaiah 61 announcing His ministry, one of the descriptions of His mission was "recovery of sight to the blind." This can refer to those spiritually blind, but we know Jesus healed those who were physically blind as well (see Matthew 9:27–30; Mark 8:22–25). Healing the sick, performing miracles, even raising the dead made up a major portion of Jesus' ministry to the people. He also preached the Gospel of the Kingdom and cast out demons.

Then He made a radical statement to His disciples: "He who believes in Me, the works that I do he will do also; and greater works than these he will do, because I go to My Father" (John 14:12). We are to believe God that we will do greater works. Only then will we demonstrate the fullness of abundant life.

God's Healing Power

Romans 8:11 declares:

> If the Spirit of Him who raised Jesus from the dead dwells in you, He who raised Christ from the dead will also give life to your mortal bodies through His Spirit who dwells in you.

We have the quickening power of God living inside us. We need only to activate it by faith in order to see healing and resurrection life.

Here are four testimonies of God's healing power to build our faith for healing.

Eddie

In chapter 6 I told the story of a pastor named Eddie who pointed his finger at me and prophesied over me, "You will preach the Word and signs will follow." It was confirmation of what God had spoken to me personally. Yet when I had shared that personal message with my pastor, he told me it could not have been the voice of God because "women don't preach."

Fast-forward almost forty years. By this time I had been in full-time ministry for 38 years and was preaching at a church in Columbus, Missouri. Toward the end of my message, who should walk into the back of the church but Brother Eddie! I paused in my message and said, "Brother Eddie, is that you?" Eddie, an older man by now, lifted up his cane, shook it at me, and called, "Preach the Word, Jane!" I still remembered his prophetic word to me all those years ago.

After I finished preaching, I called him forward and began to pray and prophesy over him. God revealed that Eddie had had an injury to his brain that God wanted to heal. Eddie said he had had several strokes and subsequent surgeries, but that he still needed healing. I asked if he had any damage in his body as a result of the strokes. He hit his left arm with his cane and said it had been hanging useless for many years, since the first stroke.

I said, "You gave me a prophetic word forty years ago that I would preach the Word and signs would follow. Tonight I activate that word and speak healing to the circuitry of your brain." Then I commanded his dead arm to come back to life.

Right in front of everyone's eyes, his left arm began to shake. Within seconds he was raising that arm and making circles. That which was dead had come back to life!

Think about this: Pastor Eddie gave me a word that changed my life. Almost forty years later, that same prophetic word changed his. It was a full-circle moment.

Carl

I was ministering with a team in upstate New York, when someone had a word of knowledge that God wanted to heal backs. Many people responded and filled the altar area, and the minister began praying for each one. Then I heard the Lord say, *I want you to go up and offer to pray only for those who have no movement in their backs—people who cannot bend at all.* I did as the Lord said, and had two older ladies come forward, whom I prayed for and watched the Lord heal.

Suddenly the congregation started pointing toward the back of the church and shouting, "Carl, Carl!" Slowly and seemingly reluctantly, a very tall man came to the front. I asked him to demonstrate his range of motion by bending over as much as he could. He could hardly bend at his waist. He had been in a motorcycle accident many years before, he explained, and had broken his back. He had had seventeen back surgeries since, even fusing some of his backbone.

The Lord whispered to me to speak directly into his eyes and to decree first the healing of his heart, then the healing of his body.

So I asked Carl to keep his eyes open and began to prophesy to him, eye to eye, as the Lord had instructed.

As I spoke to his heart, Carl began to weep. His body needed healing, but clearly God was just as concerned about his broken heart. After this I began to pray and decree to his back, releasing the healing power of Jesus Christ into his body. Then I asked him to try to bend over.

Miraculously Carl began to bend and twist. His hands reached all the way down to the floor!

God had healed his broken heart and then healed his broken back.

Marie

An elderly woman named Marie was diagnosed with stage four cancer. It had begun as an undiagnosed breast cancer and had spread to her backbone and hips. She went to the doctor in incredible pain and received a death sentence, saying she had less than a month to live. Immediately she was placed in hospice care to keep her comfortable while she died.

We were hosting healing meetings at our church with a visiting minister. Members of the church would pick up Marie from hospice and drive her to the meeting each night. She was in so much pain that she could not even sit, but had to lie down on the front chairs. And every night the visiting minister would pray for her, after which he would ask her to walk around the sanctuary. It caused her excruciating pain, but she obeyed.

After a week, the meetings were over, but she looked no better off than when they began.

Several weeks passed. Then one Sunday morning, she walked through the back doors of the church, full of life and energy. She told us she had been completely healed! Her doctors said it appeared that the cancer was somehow gone. They tried to explain it using words like *remission*, but since they had not treated her, they remained baffled by the turnaround.

Marie explained that, after she had come and received prayer each night, the next day she had gotten out of her hospice bed into a wheelchair and proceeded to go room to room in the hospice wing, praying for others. She had become a conduit of healing—and received hers as well.

Marie reconciled with her family in California, from whom she had been estranged, and moved to live near them. She lived another eight years, and when she passed away, she did not die of cancer.

John Bell

My friend John Bell serves as a missionary to Central and South America. He recounts his story of miraculous healing from terminal cancer:

On 1 October 2012, while driving in my car, my stomach perforated. I proceeded to bleed profusely from my mouth, resulting in physical death. After resuscitation, cauterization of the bleeding, and a transfusion of units of blood, I was alive and stable again. But over the next five weeks, I was diagnosed with terminal cancer.

I had a choice to make: I could choose to accept this diagnosis, become discouraged, and ultimately die. Or I could embrace the eternal life the Lord promised me in His Word. The Lord reminded me that the power of life and death are in the tongue and of His words in John 10:10.

So I gathered my family and the elders of the church to decree life over my situation. We chose to trust in the Word of God and command it to become true in this situation. We stood on top of the doctor's notes inside the intensive care unit, and spoke the words of Scripture over my body, over the diagnosis, and over my life. We declared a thing and believed that it would be established, according to Job 22:28.

I was offered palliative chemotherapy in order to possibly prolong my life for two years. Over the next five weeks, after multiple blood tests, biopsies, and prayer, the initial diagnosis of terminal cancer was miraculously changed. I finally received eight cycles of chemotherapy. Sometimes the Lord uses medicine and prayer, and we must discern His voice for our own situation.

I am still alive today, not only cancer-free but completely cured—glory to God! He truly is a miracle-working God. His miraculous power is very much alive and effective today. When it looked as if the enemy had succeeded in his plan of killing, stealing, and destroying, the Lord had the final word: *Life!*

Yes, our God is a miracle-working God!

Healing Is in the Atonement

Our God is a healing God! It is how you view healing, however, that will determine your level of faith regarding divine healing,

167

and your willingness to confront the thief to take back what he stole.

There are three views regarding healing in the Church today. Some believe that healing passed away after the first-century Church. Others believe in a "special grace" doctrine in which only some are healed, "if it's God's will." Then there are those who believe that everything written in Scripture is for today, and that healing was part of the price Christ paid when He died on the cross.

The problem is, sickness has become an accepted way of life, even for believers, who adopt the "this is just life" mentality. I reject this view. I believe it is vital to recognize that healing is in the atonement. Sickness is a corruption that we must resist, or else the thief prevails.

It is important to take care of the physical body, which is the temple of the Holy Spirit: eating right, getting plenty of sleep, not putting toxic substances in it. But when we find ourselves attacked by illness, do we adopt the "this is just life" mentality, or do we employ the quickening power of Christ to confront the thief and recover our health?

We may all have felt that some prayers regarding healing go unanswered. Perhaps you prayed for someone and that person died. Perhaps you have been believing God for your own healing, without seeing results. I do not claim to have answers as to why some people are healed and others are not. But I can encourage you that God desires to heal. He demonstrated this through the work and ministry of Jesus Christ. Otherwise Jesus would just have preached to the crowds about eternal life and saving their souls from hell, rather than demonstrating abundant life for our minds, hearts, and bodies here on this side of eternity.

In Isaiah 53:4–5 we see what Christ accomplished by going to the cross: atoning for our sin and rebellion and healing our pains and sicknesses. First let's read this passage in the New King James translation:

> Surely He has borne our griefs and carried our sorrows; yet we esteemed Him stricken, smitten by God, and afflicted. But He was wounded for our transgressions, He was bruised for our iniquities; the chastisement for our peace was upon Him, and by His stripes we are healed.

Now I will insert the meaning of some of these words, so we can better grasp the significance of Jesus' work on the cross:

- Surely He has *borne* (lifted, carried, taken away)[2]
- *Our griefs* (anxiety, disease, sickness, infirmity, pain)[3]
- And carried our *sorrows* (anguish, grief, pain, sorrow)[4]
- He was wounded for our *transgressions* (revolt, rebellion, sin, trespass)[5]
- He was bruised for our *iniquities* (perversity, evil, fault, sin,[6] depravity, guilt)[7]
- The chastisement for our *peace* (safety, wellness, happiness, welfare, health, prosperity, rest, peace, favor,[8] friendships, completeness)[9] was upon Him
- And by His stripes we are *healed* (mended, cured, healed as by a physician, repaired, made whole).[10]

Matthew 8:16–17 makes it clear that the ministry of Jesus on earth was indeed a fulfillment of Isaiah 53, bringing not only forgiveness of sins but healing:

> When evening had come, they brought to [Jesus] many who were demon-possessed. And He cast out the spirits with a word, and healed all who were sick, that it might be fulfilled which

was spoken by Isaiah the prophet, saying: "He Himself took our infirmities and bore our sicknesses."

Elsewhere in Scripture we see the power of the blood of atonement demonstrated—a prophetic picture of the power of the shed blood of Jesus Christ. Just before Israel was delivered from Egypt, the spirit of death, the final plague, was soon to be released. God told each Israelite household to kill a lamb and place its blood on the doorposts and lintels of their homes, and death would "pass over," with God saying, "No destructive plague will touch you" (Exodus 12:13 NIV). Passover is a type of the atonement of Christ. First Corinthians 5:7 says, "Christ, our Passover, was sacrificed for us."

God also kept Israel healthy when they came out of Egypt: "He led the Israelites out; they carried silver and gold, and all of them were healthy and strong" (Psalm 105:37 GNT). The King James Version uses the Hebrew word *feeble*: "There was not one feeble person among their tribes." What an incredible picture of God's sustaining power for health and well-being!

After the victory over Pharaoh's army at the Red Sea, God gave this promise:

> If you diligently heed the voice of the LORD your God and do what is right in His sight, give ear to His commandments and keep all His statutes, I will put none of the diseases on you which I have brought on the Egyptians. For I am the LORD who heals you.
>
> Exodus 15:26

God's View of Sickness

There was no sickness at creation. God did not make sickness. Genesis 1:31 says, "God saw everything that He had made, and indeed it was very good." It was Adam's sin and disobedience that caused sickness and death. According to Romans 5:12, "Sin entered the world through one man, and death through sin, and in this way death came to all people, because all sinned" (NIV). Sickness and disease are agents of death and products of our sin. They are part of the curse that entered the earth when Adam sinned. Immediate physical death did not occur, but spiritual death entered in, eventually producing natural death, including sickness and disease.

But Jesus demonstrated His dominion over every curse, including sickness, disease, and demonic powers. He came into a fallen world and healed crowds of people of whatever ailment was present. He broke the curse of sin and death. Galatians 3:13 says, "Christ has redeemed us from the curse of the law, having become a curse for us (for it is written, 'Cursed is everyone who hangs on a tree')."

Our restored dominion does not mean we will never die, since Scripture is clear: "It is appointed for men to die once" (Hebrews 9:27). But the fact that we will die does not mean we have to be sick. God's plan for abundant life for His people does not include suffering through sickness.

If you are dealing with sickness for yourself or for a loved one, please do not feel condemned. This is where we confront the thief! We first align our hearts with the truth of God's Word and choose that truth over our diagnosis or circumstance. We speak the promise rather than the problem. Then we decree God's Word, pushing back doubt and unbelief.

Supernatural Means of Healing

When we get sick, it can feel overwhelming. Fear and weariness can set in, even if we have a good biblical understanding of healing and miracles, and they can keep us from contending with spiritual weapons. So it is helpful to be empowered by the scriptural processes available to help us access healing.

To be clear, healing does not come because you do everything perfectly. You cannot earn it; it must be received. But Scripture does show us how to position ourselves to receive most effectively. Let's look at just a few of these:

1. Calling for elders to pray and anoint with oil. James 5:14–15 (KJV) says,

> Is any sick among you? let him call for the elders of the church; and let them pray over him, anointing him with oil in the name of the Lord: and the prayer of faith shall save the sick, and the Lord shall raise him up; and if he have committed sins, they shall be forgiven him.

Notice the connection between physical healing and the forgiveness of sins. Adam's sin brought sickness into the world, but Jesus offers full pardon for our sins. The prayer of the elders connects the sick person to community, authority, and faith. You do not need to fight alone.

2. Confessing faults to one another. James 5:16 continues, "Confess your faults one to another, and pray one for another, that ye may be healed" (KJV). The prayer of agreement is a powerful thing. Matthew 18:19 says, "If two of you agree on earth concerning anything that they ask, it will be done for them." The enemy's strategy is to get us fighting alone. We all need someone we trust to whom we can confess our faults.

This word *faults* refers to slip-ups, unintentional errors, willful transgressions, offenses, or trespasses.[11] Perhaps you need healing as the result of a sin. Or perhaps you are struggling in your mind. Break the power of isolation by finding someone to talk to, confessing your sin to that person, and having that person pray a prayer of agreement with you.

Once, I got sick with vertigo. It was awful. I had seen God heal the sick and even raise the dead because I had prayed, but now I could not even get out of bed. I felt weak, ashamed, and embarrassed. The enemy told me I was a fraud. After suffering for a few days, I finally told my husband how the enemy was beating me up inside and lying to me. I felt powerless. Tom prayed and broke the lie of the enemy off my mind and body. That night we met with our elders, to whom I also confessed the lies. They anointed me, prayed for me, and I was delivered in my mind and healed in my body.

I continue to pray for the sick and see them healed.

3. Speaking directly to the disease. Jesus spoke to the fig tree, and it withered. Jesus spoke to the wind and the waves, and the storm stopped. Jesus promised us that if we speak to the mountain in His name, the mountain will be removed (see Mark 11:22–24).

Once I prayed for a man with a large, life-threatening tumor in his abdomen. I spoke to the tumor, cursed it at its root, and commanded it to leave the man's body. Three days later I got word that his doctors could no longer find evidence of the tumor.

Another time we prayed for a woman who had a large, inoperable brain tumor. Her husband was a brain surgeon, yet he could not help her. We spoke to the brain tumor and commanded it to disappear. Weeks later the husband returned with film showing us the indentation in her skull where the tumor had been. It was now miraculously gone.

4. Praying in tongues. Romans 8:26 says, "The Spirit also helps in our weaknesses. For we do not know what we should pray for as we ought, but the Spirit Himself makes intercession for us with groanings which cannot be uttered." The word *weaknesses* in Greek—translated *infirmities* in the KJV—refers to feebleness, frailty, disease, sickness, weakness.[12] When we are weak or sick and do not know how to pray, we can pray in the language of the Holy Spirit, and He will help us.

In his amazing book *Sparkling Gems from the Greek*, Rick Renner says this about the help we receive from the Spirit:

> The Greek word translated "helpeth" is actually a compound of three Greek words. The first word is *sun*, meaning to do something in conjunction with someone else. The second word is *anti*, which means against. The third word is *lambano*, which means to take or to receive. When these three words are joined, the new word, *sunantilambano*, means to take hold of something with someone else, gripping it together as tightly as possible, and throwing your combined weight against it to move it out of the way. . . . It tells us that the Holy Spirit literally becomes one with us in the task of removing every obstacle. In the midst of our weaknesses, when we are inadequate to get the job done, the Holy Spirit says, "Let me grab hold of that hindrance with you, and you and I will push against it together until it is moved completely out of your way."[13]

5. Laying on of hands. Mark 16:18 says of believers, "They will lay hands on the sick, and they will recover." Tom and I once prayed and laid hands on a woman with a large lump in her breast. Within hours the lump was gone.

6. Faith-based confession and decrees. I dreamed about someone with an infection in her mouth who died. The dream was not about a person, I realized, but about how our own words can kill us. Proverbs 18:21 says, "Death and life are in the power of the tongue." And Romans 10:9–10 says:

> If you confess with your mouth the Lord Jesus and believe in your heart that God has raised Him from the dead, you will be saved. For with the heart one believes unto righteousness, and with the mouth confession is made unto salvation.

The word *saved* is the Greek word *sozo*, which means to save, deliver, protect, heal, and make whole.[14] It also implies a deliverance from the things that hinder a person from receiving all the benefits of redemption.[15]

During the COVID-19 pandemic I adapted a declaration for health and healing that I included in my book *Declarations for Breakthrough*. Many people reported a major turnaround when reading that Scripture-filled decree out loud several times a day. This decree can be personalized and adapted for specific healing needs, but it serves as a scriptural declaration to speak over your life to take back your health. Decree it with me now:

Death and life are in the power of my tongue, so I speak life over my body. It is God's will for me to be healed. It is His will that I prosper and live in health, even as my soul prospers. Jesus Christ carried my sicknesses and pains on the cross, so I do not need to carry them. By His stripes I am healed and made whole. The life is in the blood, and Jesus' shed blood makes me whole. Jesus lives in me and His life flows through me. He came to destroy the works of the devil, which include all sickness, disease, and pain; so any work of the devil in my body has already been defeated. I shall live and not die and shall declare the works of the Lord.

I command every demonic spirit of sickness, infirmity, or pain to leave my body now by the authority of the name of Jesus. He is taking all sickness from the midst of me. The thief comes to steal, kill, and destroy, but Jesus came so I could have abundant life, life that overflows with His goodness. The same Spirit that raised Christ from the dead lives in me and quickens my body to life. My body is the temple of the Holy Spirit, and all God's fullness lives in me. I will glorify Him in my body, which belongs to Him. My healing is springing forth speedily!

*A merry, joyful, happy heart is good medicine for me. I will
not forget Your benefits of forgiveness, healing, and life. Your
words impart true life and radiant health into the core of my
being. I declare that my body is completely healed now, in Jesus'
name and by the power of His Word.*[16]

7. Reading God's Word. Psalm 107:20 says, "He sent His
word and healed them, and delivered them from their destruc-
tions." Proverbs 4:22 says about the words of God, "They are
life to those who find them, and health to all their flesh." Hebrews 11:3 says that "the worlds were framed by the word of
God." Surely His Word can heal our bodies.

When I was first introduced to Spirit-filled people, I had been
diagnosed with a torn cartilage in my knee that was going to
require surgery. I met people who shared what God's Word had
to say about healing. They quoted several verses to me, which
as a young believer I had never heard. Then they said, "If He
made you, don't you think He can heal you?"

Yes, that made sense. They laid hands on me and prayed for
me, and my knee was completely healed.

8. Receiving Communion. Most non-liturgical believers receive Communion at church around once a month. It does not,
however, need to be administered by a priest or pastor; every
believer can partake of the bread and the cup in our own homes
as often as we like. It is not just something symbolic we do,
but a prophetic act of appropriation of the work of the cross.

In 1 Corinthians 11:23–30 we are instructed to partake of
Communion in remembrance of the death of Jesus Christ.
When Jesus broke the bread, He said, "This is My body which
is broken for you" (verse 24). First Peter 2:24 says, "[He] Himself bore our sins in His own body on the tree, that we, having
died to sins, might live for righteousness—by whose stripes you
were healed." In other words, His body was broken so ours can

be healed. When Jesus offered His disciples the cup of wine, He said that the wine represented His blood that would be "shed for many" for the forgiveness of sins (Matthew 26:28). Once again He was referencing the atonement for both our bodies and our souls.

Revelation 12:11 explains that believers overcome the accuser "by the blood of the Lamb and by the word of their testimony." We are given power to live in victory—physically, mentally, emotionally, and spiritually—because of what Christ did for us.

A PROPHETIC WORD FOR YOU

The Lord says to you, My child, I have seen you struggle to be free from pain and sickness. I have watched as you have suffered unnecessarily and often, even bravely, faced your trial, thinking mistakenly that it was your lot in life. I have watched as you have lived with frustration and a sense of defeat over infirmity. But My heart longs to see you receive the free gift of healing that was purchased through the blood shed by My Son, the Lord Jesus Christ. When He walked the earth and saw people in their sickness, He was moved with compassion and healed everyone.

Today I release that same yoke-breaking anointing to set you free from all pain, sickness, and disease. I break the demonic powers of physical and mental torment, and release My peace, healing, and supernatural strength into your body and mind. Receive My freedom and power to shift from sickness to health, from death to life, and from sorrow to joy. Breathe in My life and love, and let the same Spirit who raised Christ from the dead dwell in you, and quicken your body to life. (See Romans 8:11.)

A DECREE TO TAKE BACK YOUR HEALTH

[Speak this aloud in faith!] *I decree that I am taking back my health from the enemy by the power of the atonement of Jesus Christ over my life. His body was broken so mine can be healed. His blood was shed so I can be free. He wore the crown of thorns so my mind can be free. He took a spear in His side, right by His heart, so my heartache can be healed. He bore 39 lashes on His back to heal me. I receive healing, therefore, in every area of my body and mind.*

My body will function as it was created to, healed from any illness or disease. My mind will be sharp and clear, free from oppression. It is God's will for me to be healed. Jesus bore my sorrow and carried my grief on the cross. Therefore, I will not carry the burden of my sickness, disease, anxiety, weakness, or mental or physical pain. I give those to Jesus and thank Him for carrying them for me. I command all those infirmities to leave my body, my mind, and my life, in Jesus' name. I will be strong and healthy. I will live in divine health. I will have joy instead of sorrow. I choose life today, and declare that the same Spirit who raised Christ from the dead dwells in me and is quickening my mortal body and bringing victory. I believe it and I decree it, in the mighty name of Jesus.

QUESTIONS TO CONSIDER

1. What areas of your life need God's healing touch?
2. Which of the biblical approaches to healing have you used to receive healing from the Lord?
3. Which of the biblical approaches to healing have you not yet utilized to receive healing in your life?

4. Are there any areas of physical, emotional, or mental sickness in which you have given up hope of receiving your healing? If so, can you think of one testimony of healing, either from your past or one you have heard another person share, that you can speak aloud or share with another person? This testimony, according to Revelation 12:11, becomes a weapon in your mouth to overcome the accuser.

5. Write a decree, or modify one of the decrees I have provided, that addresses specific healing needs you have. Speak this daily as part of your devotional time.

NINE

TAKING BACK OUR PASSION

Who knows whether you have come to the kingdom for such a time as this?

Esther 4:14

A ll our previous chapters have dealt with how the Amalekites, the robbers, waged war on God's people. Each Old Testament battle was leading to the final confrontation with that lineage—an all-or-nothing, winner-take-all fight. This conflict between God's people and the thief came to an explosive conclusion in the book of Esther.

Although the lineage of Amalekite robbers was cut off in that day, we are still dealing with the spiritual forces today that seek to steal, kill, and destroy. Perhaps you have been in a confrontation with the thief in some area of your life. Perhaps you have been contending for your health, your family, your purpose, your finances, your peace, or your prophetic promise. The story of Esther heralds our ultimate victory over the robber and ushers in a time of divine recovery, a boomerang season, when everything the enemy has tried to use against us is turned back on his own head!

Haman's Vendetta

In the spring of 474 BC,[1] the streets of Shushan, the capital city of the Persian Empire, were buzzing over the latest decree issued throughout the land. Haman, King Ahasuerus' chief minister, had proclaimed that eleven months from that time, all the Jews in the kingdom were to be killed and their property seized for the royal court.

Haman had been enraged by Mordecai, a Jewish official serving in the king's court, who had escalated the fight when he refused to bow in homage to Haman. The king had commanded all in the land to bow down and "reverence" Haman, a word that in Hebrew carries the meaning of worship.[2] Righteous Mordecai knew he had to refuse to give in to Persian idolatry, remaining separate. But this infuriated Haman. He also hated the Jews, Mordecai's people, and was seeking to settle old ancestral scores, as he came from the lineage of Agag, the Amalekite king killed by the Hebrew prophet Samuel.

So Haman had proclaimed that all the Jews in the kingdom were to be killed and their property seized. He was out for the ultimate spoil, not only stripping the Jews of their possessions but completely cutting off the Jewish heritage.

His devious mind had concocted a plan to cast lots for the best day to accomplish this heinous act (which was an occult practice of the day), and he had scheduled the slaughter for a specific day the following year. He spread the proclamation throughout the land so the Jews could spend their final months in fear, anxiety, and distress.

Haman is a picture of our mortal enemy, the devil, the thief, who comes to steal, kill, and destroy. Although the devil was defeated when Jesus Christ died on the cross and rose again, he still has a vendetta against God's people. He wants to make them suffer as much as possible and rob them of everything that is good. Like Haman, however, the thief has forgotten that God is on our side and that the battle is won before it ever gets started.

As a response to this evil decree, Mordecai changed out of his prestigious garments into sackcloth and ashes and went weeping and wailing throughout the city all the way to the king's gate. Following his example, Jews in every province donned the same mourning clothes and raised a cry of distress. The nation was in an uproar. The enemy was advancing and God's people were in peril. (It can feel similar today, but don't lose heart!)

More than a century earlier, the Jews had been carried into captivity from their homeland in Judah. Then, after a seventy-year period of exile, Cyrus the Great decreed that the Jews might return to resettle Jerusalem, rebuild the Temple, which had been destroyed, and reestablish Temple worship. Many returned. Others remained settled throughout the 127 provinces of the Persian Empire and were now occupying positions in society and government. But they had not assimilated into Persian culture. Mordecai, when commanded to bow down and honor wicked Haman, stood his ground boldly and refused to compromise his faith.

So Haman determined to wipe out all Jews living anywhere in the provinces of Persia. His decree was designed to annihilate God's people and their influence in the land and culture of the day. He had declared war on righteousness and on the people who refused to bow down to idolatrous structures. All the while, pressure was mounting on the Jews to compromise their spiritual principles and hide their spiritual identity. It was the ultimate in "cancel culture." At every turn it seemed as though the wicked were prospering and the righteous were being persecuted. Only a divine reversal could save them.

The release of this decree of death set the stage for one of the most triumphant stories in biblical history. The account of victory found in the book of Esther has brought hope to God's people time and again through the ages in times of persecution and distress. It tells the story of an orphan girl who became queen of the greatest empire of that day and how God used her to overturn the decree of the enemy and save a nation. It shows how God takes what the enemy plans for evil and turns it for good.

But although it sounds romantic, it was no Cinderella story.

Dethroning Vashti

Several years prior to Haman's decree, another earth-shaking decree had been released from the king's palace. The king had taken the royal crown from his wife, Vashti, and was now in search of a new queen.

What happened to cause the king to make such a drastic decision against his beautiful, powerful wife? The first chapter of Esther tells us that the king had been throwing a banquet for all the leaders of the provinces in his kingdom, a banquet that lasted 180 days. Vashti was throwing her own banquet for the women. At the end of this time, the king commanded Vashti to present herself, wearing her royal crown, to show her beauty to the leaders. She refused, and the king was furious. After a period of deliberation, he decided to strip Vashti of her royal crown and give it "to another who is better than she" (Esther 1:19).

Now, in response to his search for a new queen, Esther had to answer a summons to present herself to the court of the king, just like the most beautiful virgins of the land. She had to lay aside her hopes and dreams for love and marriage. If she was selected, she would be made queen. If not, she would be kept as part of the king's harem, with no life or love of her own.

If Esther is an example of the modern Church that is obedient to God's call, Vashti is quite the opposite. She is an example of those who have been part of God's Kingdom, who are beautiful, positioned, and powerful, yet who have chosen complacency, disobedience, and a disdain for the presence of the King. Sadly, many claiming to represent Christendom in the earth reflect the indifferent nature of Vashti rather than the passion of Esther.

Vashti contains all the beauty of the religious Church, but she no longer has a passion to obey her King or to be in His presence. In truth, she no longer respects His sovereignty. His Word is no longer preeminent. She decides what is right and wrong for herself.

In the same way, many who gather in the name of Christianity have become like Vashti. Many churches no longer acknowledge God's Word as truth, but make up their own rules as they go along. Some no longer accept Jesus Christ as the only way to the Father, believing instead that there are many paths to heaven. They have a form of Christianity, but not the truth, power, or manifestation of the Holy Spirit.

This, too, is the result of the spirit of robbery—taking away the truth of the Gospel, undermining the power of the Holy Spirit, and compromising all that Jesus laid His life down to provide for us.

In the story of Esther, the king chose her as his new queen and placed the crown on her head.

As I studied this account, I heard the Lord say, *I am taking the crown of favor off those groups and searching the earth for those who will be part of My Esther Church, those who are willing to obey Me. I am looking for those who delight in*

My presence and who honor My words. I am empowering My Esther Church to push back against the gates of hell and take back all that the enemy has stolen. I am seeking those who will love Me and My Kingdom first, above their own comfort, even above their own lives.

Once I was on an airplane, reading a book with a Christian title, while seated next to a man reading a book with what also seemed to be a spiritual title, so we struck up a conversation. I shared that my husband and I were pastors. He replied that he was also a pastor. So I asked him the name of his church.

"The Christian Church," he replied.

"What does your church believe?"

"Oh, we're a nondoctrinal church."

I laughed, thinking he was trying to be funny. "Can you do that?"

"No, really," he said. "We don't preach doctrine. We just preach love."

I could see where this conversation was going, so I said, "Yes, preaching love is good, but surely with a name like 'The Christian Church,' you believe that Jesus is the only way to heaven?"

My fellow passenger rolled his eyes. "You sound like a Baptist!"

He meant it as an insult, but I took it as a compliment.

"So you don't believe Jesus is the only way to the Father?" I asked.

"No, we believe there are many paths to God."

I replied, quoting John 14:6, "What about when Jesus said, 'I am the way, the truth and the life. No one comes to the Father except through Me'?"

"When the disciples wrote the gospels," he replied, "they wrote using poetic speech."

I was not familiar with this term or what he meant by it. So he explained, "It's as if I were to tell you that my wife is the most beautiful woman on earth. I know in reality that she is not, but out of my love for her, I might make extravagant, poetic statements about her. The disciples did the same out of their love for Christ. But in reality, Jesus, as wonderful as He is, is only one of the paths to God."

Wow! To believe as this man did would mean discounting the entirety of Scripture, making it fit a religious construct of our own making. Whether he would admit it or not, although he had said he pastored a nondoctrinal church, he definitely preached doctrine—only it was false doctrine.

It is the doctrine of a Vashti Church that, sadly, many groups have adopted in order to be more inclusive. These churches may use the term *Christian* to describe themselves, but their teachings have little to do with the Bible, and their gatherings have little to do with coming into the presence of the King or obeying His commands. Sadly, they have become like Vashti: beautiful, entertaining, but comfortable in their complacency, disinterested in any royal responsibility or assignment.

But Vashti is being dethroned and her crown is being given to another who is better than she.

"Update or Vacate"

The days of casual, comfortable Christianity are finished. An Esther Church is arising that knows who we are and whom we serve. We have Kingdom assignments to accomplish as we follow Jesus, the King. Like Esther, we recognize that we have "come to the kingdom for such a time as this" (Esther 4:14). Our crown of favor and authority is not just for meeting our own needs, but about utilizing our spiritual positioning to make a difference in the earth. Like Esther, we are positioned for a purpose. The scepter of favor extended to us—a life-saving act of God's grace that we will discuss shortly—is not about us but about overturning the decrees the enemy has made against our families, our churches, our communities, and our nations. God has positioned us to turn what is upside down, right side up!

We are living in the day when God is pouring out His Spirit on all who call on His name and are seeking Him, whether they attend a historic denominational church or a more modern congregation. Eyes are being opened to the truth. Hearts are being set ablaze by the fire of the Holy Spirit. Revival is stirring across the nations as the lost are being saved and lives are being transformed from dead, dry religion to the fullness of all God intended, living life in the power of the Spirit.

I once had a dream in which an angel told me there was a fresh outpouring of God's Spirit coming on the historic denominational churches that had lost their way, just like the man I talked with on the plane. It would be much like the charismatic renewal of the 1960s and '70s, the angel said, in which mainstream Christianity would receive the baptism of the Holy Spirit and a passion for the truth of God's Word. This outpouring, said the angel, would give these churches the opportunity to "update or vacate" their denominations.

I knew the term *update* did not mean to develop some extra-biblical doctrine of humanism and inclusion, but rather, as 2 Peter 1:12 says, to be "established in the present truth." This means walking in the fullness of all God has restored in biblical truth over the last several centuries, whether it be embracing salvation by grace through faith, holiness, physical healing, the baptism of the Holy Spirit with the evidence of speaking in other tongues, the gifts of the Spirit, apostolic and prophetic understanding, and more. These were all doctrines restored from Scripture during the Protestant Reformation.

God is reforming us once again, that we might represent Christ's original intent—that, in the words of Matthew 16:18

(KJV), "the gates of hell shall not prevail against" His Church. The word we use for *Church* is *ekklesia*, which was not a spiritual term, but a governmental and military term of the day. The *ekklesia* was the Greek assembly, those called to rule. In Rome the *ekklesia* was a military task force called to bring transformation to territories.

Jesus' Church was never meant to be a social club, although His people find a sense of family. It was never supposed to be a humanitarian aid station, although part of the power of transformation comes through charitable works and caring for the poor. It was never supposed to be a self-help therapy group, although people find healing for their souls. It was never supposed to be a place of entertainment, although people use their gifts to bring glory to the King.

No, we were designed to be the *ekklesia*, the place of spiritual legislation, the house of worship and warfare, the people of authority and power to open the heavens and shift the earth. Like Esther, we are to be a people who revoke every decree of death and destruction issued by hell, and release heaven's decrees of freedom and blessing into the earth.

Mordecai, Watchman Reformer

We have already noted that Haman was from the lineage of Agag, the king of the Amalekites. This race of giants had stolen God's prophetic promise for the Israelites to possess the land, trying to intimidate them from crossing over to take possession. They pillaged the threshing floors of harvest in the time of Gideon. They stole from David and his men, taking their wives and children and all their possessions at Ziklag.

But in each of these scenarios, the Jews found faith in their God, rose up, and took back all that was stolen. Each time, the evil plans against God's people boomeranged back on the heads of the Amalekites. With every battle, Israel got back more than was stolen.

The same kind of turnaround occurred in the days of Esther, as we will see. She and Mordecai represent the one-two punch of the watchman and the intercessor. These are reformation anointings that bring breakthrough according to God's divine purpose, defeating the plans of the enemy.

If we are going to experience victory, we must learn to do as Jesus instructed us and to watch and pray. At His critical hour, just before His arrest, His disciples were supposed to be praying for Him—but instead He found them sleeping. Jesus admonished them, "What! Could you not watch with Me one hour? Watch and pray, lest you enter into temptation. The spirit indeed is willing, but the flesh is weak" (Matthew 26:40–41).

Much of the Church is sleeping while the enemy is killing, stealing, and destroying. Ephesians 6:18 challenges us to "[pray] always with all prayer and supplication in the Spirit, being watchful." The word *watchful* in the Greek means to stay awake and watch,[3] to be circumspect, attentive, and ready, to exercise constant vigilance over something.[4] We need to not just think about watching and praying but to actually answer Jesus' call to watch and pray. We need to be intentional. We need to answer His call to be watchmen in this critical hour in history.

Mordecai, Esther's cousin, was a watchman. In Old Testament times, watchmen were stationed on the walls or watchtowers of the city, on hilltops to watch over the harvest, or at the gates of access in the city (see Proverbs 8:34–35; Isaiah 62:6; Jeremiah 31:6). Mordecai sat at the gate of the city as a spiritual father and government official. He was recognized as a father in the land, which was an apostolic and prophetic oversight role for the people.

In the natural realm, this fatherhood anointing was evident as he took in his orphaned cousin Esther and raised her as his own daughter, in righteousness. And as a watchman, he was able to help Esther get into position to become the queen in a pagan land. Watchmen-prophet-reformers help get the *ekklesia* and its members into place to effect change in the earth.

As a watchman, Mordecai was able to expose the plans of two men who planned on assassinating the king, thus saving his life (see Esther 2:21–22). Watchmen are positioned to see both the natural and the spiritual devices of the enemy to prevent his plans from succeeding.

As a watchman, Mordecai also guarded and assessed the spiritual condition of the Jewish people, sounding the alarm in the face of compromise. Numbers of Jews may have attended the king's lavish banquet in the first chapter of Esther, where leaders ate and drank for 180 days. And later, when the king commanded everyone in the land to bow down and "reverence" Haman, Mordecai refused to bow—but we are not told that any others defied the order.

As a watchman and reformer, Mordecai had become aware of the subtle slide of compromise in the spiritual lives of the Jews. Rather than maintain their distinction as a counter-culture, God's chosen people, they were slowly assimilating and becoming a subculture in Persia.

Watchmen have the responsibility to raise the standard of righteousness and to cry out for holiness, revival, and the fear of the Lord to burn in the hearts of God's people. We must be a distinct people, not giving in to the idolatry and deception in the world. We must watch and pray over our own souls, and also over the soul of our nation.

What was the response of Mordecai, the watchman, the reformer, upon hearing of the decree of death and destruction? Before any plan or strategy was formed, he humbled himself with sackcloth and ashes and wept in the streets. He was weeping over wickedness. He was weeping over what seemed to be the enemy prevailing. He was weeping over his nation.

As watchmen today, are we weeping for the lost? Are we crying out for those whom the devil is tormenting? Are we contending spiritually for our nation? Those around us are being taken captive by the devil and, unless they turn to Christ, will spend eternity in hell. Does that touch our hearts?

As watchmen, we cannot afford to harden our hearts to the plight of men and women all around us. We have a responsibility to watch, both in the natural and spiritual realms, to see heaven's plans as well as the plans of hell. We are called to cry out for awakening, revival, and harvest. If not us, then who will watch and pray?

As watchmen, we must see the big picture regarding the spiritual battles we face. Mordecai understood what was at stake in dealing with Haman. This was a final showdown, a winner-take-all battle.

In chapter 6 we saw that the prophet Samuel gave Saul, king of Israel, God's instructions regarding the upcoming battle with the Amalekites. The Lord of Hosts wanted Saul to punish them for how they had treated Israel when they came out of Egypt. Saul's assignment, as outlined in 1 Samuel 15, was to utterly destroy them—men, women, children, animals, everything— because God's judgment had already been passed upon them. Saul failed to do that. Eventually Agag was taken captive and Samuel himself killed him—but not before some of his descendants went free.

Haman was a descendant of Agag. But Mordecai and Esther were descendants of Saul, the son of Kish (see Esther 2:5–6 and 1 Samuel 9:3). Mordecai was watching over God's eternal purposes. He knew God was appointing His people to finish what his ancestor Saul had failed to do more than five hundred years earlier. Either the Jews would prevail and wipe out Amalek, or else Haman would prevail and utterly destroy them. So Mordecai urged his cousin, Esther, to approach the king and ask for the lives of their people.

We are living in such a critical time. The devil would love to see those who stand for Christ completely pushed out of the public square. He would love to silence the voice of righteousness in government, education, and business. Every day, in every form of media, we see unflattering depictions of Christians, in many instances framed as the bad guy. Those who believe in biblical morality are "canceled," often losing positions, jobs, and influence. Haman is alive and well, assassinating the character of the Church and attempting to wipe out our influence in nations once and for all.

It is time for a divine reversal and a recovery of the reputation of the Church. Can such a turnaround occur? It happened in Esther's day. If God did it then, He can do it again!

Esther, Intercessor

Esther was the pivotal character in this epic battle between Haman and his descendants and the Jews. We know she answered the challenge of Mordecai to intervene, intercede, and fulfill the call of God on her life.

The word *intercede* has several meanings, one of which is "to get between."[5] Esther got between Haman's plan and her own people. Our mission as the Esther Church is the same. We must get between and in the way of the enemy's plan to steal, kill, and destroy. We must learn to employ the same spiritual graces Esther used to accomplish our task of turning hearts and nations back to God.

The only way the death decree of Haman could be countered was for Esther to make a successful appeal to the king for her people. She would need to present herself boldly to the king—who did not know she was one of the Jews Haman planned to kill—to make her appeal. The problem was, he had not summoned her for thirty days. And anyone who approached him without being summoned, unless the king chose to extend his golden scepter, would die. So if Esther did not find the king's favor, it would cost her her life.

But when Esther appeared before the king, he did extend his scepter of favor and asked for her request—and then granted it, as we will see.

As believers we have access to the heavenly throne room. But we must recognize that the accuser of the brethren also stands before the throne of God, defaming the righteous "day and night" (Revelation 12:10). He tries to disqualify, shame, and weaken us in our relationship with God. If he can convince us that we do not have the favor of our King, we will back up and fail to answer God's challenge to boldness.

But through Christ, God is extending His scepter toward us as we come boldly before His throne of grace (favor), "that we may obtain mercy and find grace to help in time of need" (Hebrews 4:16). We can make our appeal to the King to show us favor and bring a reversal of the works of the enemy. He is granting us favor, just as the Persian king granted favor to Esther. But we must spend it wisely to open the right doors for the cause of God's Kingdom.

Boomerang Season

Esther 7 describes the uncovering of Haman's plot. The king, furious to learn that his queen was one of the Jews in his kingdom decreed for death, ordered Haman's execution on the very gallows Haman had built to hang his enemy, Mordecai. He then gave Esther possession of "the house of Haman" (Esther 8:1). This means she now owned all the property, possessions, and wealth previously owned by Haman. Haman's sons had thus been dispossessed of their inheritance, which was probably substantial, since Haman was second only to the king in the land.

Notice that when the spirit of Haman is overthrown, the Esther Church possesses all that was once his. There is a wealth transfer, along with new authority over property and possessions.

The death of Haman was a great victory for Esther and Mordecai, but only the beginning of freedom for God's people. You see, Haman was dead, but his decree was not, and neither were his ten sons, who were probably now seeking vengeance against Esther for the loss of their father and their inheritance.

In the introduction to this book, I wrote that the Lord awakened me one night to say, *It is time for the hanging of Haman's ten sons.* Immediately I began studying the book of Esther again, noting several interesting things. For one thing, I wondered why the Bible provides the names of each of Haman's ten sons. Did each of those names contain a demonic assignment to try to continue to rob the people of God? We will explore this in the very next chapter.

But for now, Haman's decree still authorized the murder of all Jews. In those days in Persia, when the king signed and sealed a decree, it was impossible to reverse it. Something more had to be done to stop the slaughter of the Jews. Haman was dead, but Esther could not give up or back off. She had to press the battle to the full.

So she went before the king again to ask for favor, which he granted. Because he could not reverse the decree that had been written, he ordered Esther and Mordecai:

> Now write another decree in the king's name in behalf of the
> Jews as seems best to you, and seal it with the king's signet

ring—for no document written in the king's name and sealed with his ring can be revoked.

Esther 8:8 NIV

So Esther and Mordecai called for the scribes and wrote a different decree, giving the people of God the authority to fight back and turn it around. They would no longer be helpless or hopeless regarding their future. This new decree empowered them to prepare for the day of battle and then engage, knowing the power of the throne was with them.

In Esther 9 we read the entire story of reversal. Instead of the defeat of the Jews at the hand of Haman and his ten sons and their Persian allies, the reverse occurred. The Jews fought back and won a great victory. They took two days wiping out the opposition, then stopped and had a big party. They went from trial to triumph, from victims to victors.

In a final note of victory, Esther asked the king for the ten sons of Haman to be hanged on the gallows Haman had prepared for Mordecai, on which he himself had been executed.

> Haman son of Hammedatha, the Agagite, the archenemy of all Jews, had schemed to destroy all Jews. He had cast the *pur* (the lot) to throw them into a panic and destroy them. But when Queen Esther intervened with the king, he gave written orders that the evil scheme that Haman had worked out should *boomerang back on his own head*. He and his sons were hanged on the gallows. That's why these days are called "Purim," from the word *pur* or "lot."
>
> Esther 9:24–26 MSG, emphasis added

As a result of Esther's intervention with the king, the last of the Amalekites were destroyed, their natural lineage wiped from the face of the earth. The schemes of the enemy boomeranged back on their own heads.

Yet in Exodus 17:16, Moses said that "the LORD will have war with Amalek from generation to generation." Today our battle is not against a natural foe, but a spiritual one, who is just as determined to harass, torment, and rob God's people. As we study Queen Esther's intervention and the assistance given by Mordecai, we gain strategies for complete victory and divine recovery of all that has been taken.

Answering the Call

The story of Esther is the story of grit, self-sacrifice, and determination not to allow evil to win. It is the story of vision, bravery, and submission to a Kingdom cause above one's own heart or desires. It is a story about us, God's Church, a "now" word for God's people everywhere not to give in to the pressures of compromise and conformity. We are not to give up our ground of righteousness and justice, for these are the very foundations of God's throne in the earth. We must become the people who, like Esther and Mordecai, are willing to stand in the face of impossible odds and fight to take back what the enemies of godliness have stolen. We fight not just for ourselves but for our nations and for future generations.

Today the Church, like Esther, is answering God's call to stand against the wicked decrees of the devil and to take back nations and generations. Many, like Esther, have been spiritual orphans, without a heritage, who are connected to their Mordecai and have been positioned through Christ to make a difference in the earth. God is raising up unlikely candidates to become great deliverers and world-changers, as they stand up for what is right.

Just as Esther went through a time of preparation and purification before she was chosen as queen, so God has been purifying the hearts and lives of believers through the Holy Spirit, strengthening them to resist the encroaching evil in the land. These know how to receive and utilize God's anointing, not to meet their own needs for comfort and prosperity, but for divine favor for earthly assignments. When Esther was faced with a kingdom crisis, her response was, "If I perish, I perish!" (Esther 4:16). These are those willing to sacrifice all, doing whatever it takes to see the enemy defeated and God's purposes advanced.

This Esther Church understands intercession and how we must come boldly before the throne of the King to see evil and corruption defeated. We understand, just as Esther did, that it is our mission to bring the life, peace, and justice of Christ into our land, even in the face of great wickedness. This is a story of divine recovery.

Open Your Mouth and Decree

Jesus told His disciples that the gates of hell "shall not prevail against" His *ekklesia* (Matthew 16:18 kjv). *Prevail* is the Greek word *katischuo*, which means to overpower.[6] Jesus was not saying the gates of hell do not have power; He was saying that His power is greater. When the enemy makes a decree against us, Jesus was saying that, like the decree of Esther and Mordecai, our godly decree supersedes the power of the enemy's decree.

When the Lord told me, *It is time for the hanging of Haman's ten sons*, and I began studying the book of Esther again, I noted that it was on the twenty-third day of Sivan that Esther and Mordecai wrote the new decree authorizing the Jews to fight back (see Esther 8:9). What day, I wondered, would correspond with that date on our Roman calendar? Was I ever surprised to find that the twenty-third of Sivan that year was June 21, the very day I was looking it up! I knew at that moment that this was a now word for the Church and that things were getting ready to shift.

Sometimes we may feel as if we are fighting a losing battle because the enemy has made decrees against our lives that seem to be in full effect. The enemy's decree may sound like this: "Failure, shame, poverty, disease, premature death, depression, oppression, heaviness, sorrow . . ." He loves to declare darkness over God's people. But Jesus came to destroy every curse. He empowers us to speak to every mountain of opposition or oppression and command it to be cast into the sea, and it will obey us! Sometimes we are waiting on God to deliver us, when actually He is waiting for us to open our mouths and make a decree.

If you identify something the enemy has decreed, open your mouth and make a different decree. Regardless of how hopeless your situation may seem, know that your decree, like Esther's, will get in the way of the enemy's plans and flip the script.

The Lord spoke to me once and decreed a season of divine reversals. During the next couple of years, we saw blind eyes see, deaf ears hear, prodigals turn around and come home, lawsuits settled with favor, bankruptcy reversed, even divorce turned around for miraculous reconciliation. It was a turnaround season then. It is a turnaround season now.

Revival Is at Hand

The decree Esther and Mordecai wrote, authorizing the Jews to fight back, was sent to all the provinces in the land. Then something miraculous began to happen:

> In each and every province and in each and every city, wherever the king's command and his decree arrived, the Jews celebrated with gladness and joy, a feast and a holiday. And many among the peoples of the land became Jews, for the fear of the Jews [and their God] had fallen on them.

Esther 8:17 AMP

Did you catch that? Hearts began to turn and revival broke out! The citizens who were previously on the side of Haman, ready to help slaughter the Jews, experienced the fear of the Lord and converted to Judaism. In that day, that was revival!

Get ready to see the fear of the Lord released in our day that will turn some of the hardest hearts to the Lord. Romans 11:22 says, "Behold therefore the goodness and severity of God" (KJV). Some people are saved because God's love, mercy, and goodness lead them to repentance. Others experience the fear of the Lord regarding hell and His severity in dealing with the unrepentant sinner. When I poll my audiences about what led them to receive Christ as Savior, it is generally about half and half.

In this season of awakening and revival, we must preach the full Gospel message—not just John 3:16, "For God so loved the world that He gave His only begotten Son, that whoever believes in Him should not perish but have everlasting life," but also John 3:18, "He who believes in Him is not condemned; but he who does not believe is condemned already, because he has not believed in the name of the only begotten Son of God." God is both goodness and severity. If we preach only half the Gospel, we will reap only half the harvest. Revival is at hand!

A Turnaround Season

Not only did Persia begin to experience revival, but the government, which had been set against the Jews, turned around as well:

> Even all the officials of the provinces and the chief rulers (satraps) and the governors and those who attended to the king's business supported the Jews [in defeating their enemies], because the fear of Mordecai [and his God's power] had fallen on them.
>
> Esther 9:3 AMP

As hostile as governments and laws have been toward God's people in our day, God is looking for Mordecai watchmen and Esther intercessors to arise and take their place. It is time for the Esther Church to make her decrees and join the spiritual fight. It is time for the hanging of Haman and his ten sons— the plunderers, conspirators, and murderers. It is time for a turnaround in the nations. If God did it then, in that hostile land, He can do it again today.

A PROPHETIC WORD FOR YOU

The Lord says, *Where are My Esthers who will answer the call of intercession to see nations and generations saved? Where are My Mordecais who will watch and pray to see decrees of darkness exposed and demonic assignments broken? I am delivering you from every spirit of fear and intimidation that has tried to hold you back. I am removing Vashti's garments of the spirits of religion and compromise, and mantling you instead with the royal robes of truth and righteousness. I am placing a crown of authority on your head and extending My scepter of favor to you. I am filling you with courage and a sense of prophetic purpose, for I have brought you to the Kingdom for this time and this hour. Rise up, Esther, and write new decrees for the future, overturning the decrees of death and destruction. Rise up, Mordecai, and rule and legislate by My Spirit. It is time for victory over the spirit of Haman and his sons, a time for victory over robbery and a time for recovering all.*

A DECREE FOR THE ESTHER CHURCH

[Speak this aloud in faith!] *I decree that the Esther Church is arising in power, wisdom, and great authority in the earth. I will be bold and make my appeal before the throne of the King. I decree that every plot and scheme of Haman, the thief, is being exposed, and that he will be hanged on the very gallows he built to defeat me. This is a boomerang season in which the curse is being turned to a blessing for me because the Lord loves me. This is my time of divine reversal. It is my time of divine recovery. It is my time of revival.*

I receive the extended scepter of favor, and will use that favor not just for personal gain but for Kingdom advancement. It is a history-making hour of governmental turnaround. It is time for the hanging of Haman's ten sons. This is my hour of victory. In Jesus' mighty name I decree it!

QUESTIONS TO CONSIDER

1. Are you a Vashti or an Esther? If you have made a decision to embrace all that God is doing, write, "I am an Esther."

2. Have you answered God's call of bravery to see the decrees of the enemy overturned? Can you recognize any of those decrees working against your life? If so, write a new decree.

3. Were you saved because of the message of the love of God or because the fear of the Lord came upon you?

4. How will you pray for your nation now that you have accepted the call of Esther? Is there any area of spiritual, political, or governmental involvement into which God is calling you?

5. Are you believing for any specific area of your life to experience God's divine reversal anointing? God's scepter is extended to you. Write a decree and speak it out loud.

TEN

THE HANGING OF
HAMAN'S TEN SONS

When Queen Esther intervened with the king, he gave written orders that the evil scheme that Haman had worked out should boomerang back on his own head. He and his sons were hanged on the gallows. That's why these days are called "Purim."

Esther 9:25–26 MSG

We have reached the epic final Old Testament conflict between the Jews and their archenemies, the Amalekites. It culminates in the battle between the Jews, led by Esther and Mordecai, and Haman, a descendant of the Amalekite king Agag and his ten sons.

Haman has long been a representation of pure evil to the Jewish people because of his conspiracy to destroy them. He wrote decrees of death and destruction against them, even circling a day on the calendar when the slaughter would take place. He had an ancient score to settle with the people with whom his lineage had waged war for centuries.

When Hitler was in power in the twentieth century, Jewish communities called him Haman, for his similar plans to exterminate them. He even cast himself as Haman in a January 30, 1944, radio speech, saying that if Nazi Germany did not prevail, the Jews could celebrate a second triumphant Purim festival.[1] It became illegal for Jews to read the book of Esther during Hitler's time in power.

Christians take it another step and recognize Haman as an example of the devil, the thief, and the antichrist spirit (meaning "against Christ" or "against the anointing"). Haman is an enemy of righteous leaders, both in the religious culture and for those who dare to stand up for righteousness in the public square, as Mordecai did. As in the story of Esther, God is raising up people bold enough to confront the thief and see the overturning of every decree of death and assignment of destruction against God's people.

The Completed Work

In the last chapter, we saw that Mordecai challenged Esther to go before the king to seek the reversal of Haman's decree, even though approaching the king when not summoned could cost her life. She answered the call and went before the throne to make her petition. What Esther did, when she found favor from the king, was to request that he and Haman join her for a banquet.

After the first successful dinner, she made a second request for the king and Haman to attend another dinner in their honor. This time she revealed her heritage as a Jew as well as Haman's plot to kill her people.

The king was outraged and stepped outside to consider his options—during which time Haman fell across Esther's couch, begging for his life. When the king stepped back into the room, it looked as though Haman was attacking his queen, and the furious Ahasuerus immediately had Haman hanged on the gallows Haman himself had built to hang Mordecai. It was the beginning of the boomerang plan, when the evil meant against the Jews bounced back on their enemy.

But Esther had to approach the king's throne once again for favor. Remember, Haman was dead but his decree was not. It still had the force of the king's seal upon it and could not be reversed. And it still empowered every person who hated God's people—including Haman's ten sons—with the authority to carry out the destruction on the day appointed.

The king extended his scepter of favor once again, instructing Esther and Mordecai to write a new decree authorizing the Jewish people to fight back against their enemy. So on the appointed day, the Jews—and those touched by the fear of the Lord and siding with them—destroyed their would-be destroyers, killing thousands in self-defense, including Haman's ten sons.

Esther then made a strange request of the king. She asked that Haman's ten sons all be hanged on public display. The king granted her request, recognizing that in ancient times, when you hung the body of your vanquished enemy on display, you were declaring to all who followed that leader, "His rule is over. He no longer has authority. He has been defeated. Beware of trying to follow in his footsteps." This warning completed the work.

Recovery Agents

When Jesus came to earth, died on the cross, and rose again, He vanquished hell and destroyed the works of the enemy. He did not hang the bodies of the devil or his demons, as they are disembodied spirits, but He did display them as vanquished foes throughout the spirit world. Colossians 2:14–15 (TPT, emphasis added) declares:

> He canceled out every legal violation we had on our record and the old arrest warrant that stood to indict us. He erased it all—our sins, our stained soul—he deleted it all and they cannot be retrieved! Everything we once were in Adam has been placed onto his cross and nailed permanently there as a public display of cancellation.
>
> Then Jesus made a public spectacle of all the powers and principalities of darkness, stripping away from them every weapon and all their spiritual authority and power to accuse us. And by the power of the cross, Jesus led them around as prisoners in a procession of triumph. *He was not their prisoner; they were his!*

Jesus destroyed the destroyer! He was sending this message to the spirit realm: "This foe is defeated. He has no authority. His rule is over."

So why are we still battling a defeated foe? Why do we still have to contend with the devil in our daily lives? Why must we still wage a spiritual war? Why does it still seem that our enemy has power?

Even though Jesus' work was complete—He disempowered our enemy and sealed the devil's fate to be thrown into the lake of fire at the end of the age—He left us the honor of enforcing "the written judgment" against him (Psalm 149:9).

In 1 Peter 5:8 we are warned, "Be of sober spirit, be on the alert. Your adversary, the devil, prowls around like a roaring lion, seeking someone to devour" (NASB). Again in Ephesians 6:11–12, we are told to put on "the whole armor of God" so we can stand against all the wiles, tactics, and schemes of the devil. Paul warns us that we are not wrestling with flesh and blood (people) "but against principalities, against powers, against the rulers of the darkness of this age, against spiritual hosts of wickedness in the heavenly places." As in Esther, the enemy is defeated but his demonic hordes continue to roam the earth seeking to steal, kill, and destroy. Clearly there is still a battle to fight against evil forces that remain.

I once heard the Lord say He was anointing His people to be "recovery agents" against evil. Looking up this term, I recalled that when a criminal is arrested, he can often pay a bail bond to gain release from jail until the court date. If he fails to show up in court, he is considered a fugitive from the law. A recovery agent (or bounty hunter) is then employed to track down the fugitive until an arrest can be made and the fugitive brought before the court for judgment.[2]

This is our function as members of God's *ekklesia*. We are to track down the places where the fugitive, our defeated enemy, has been hiding, and bring him before the court of the King for justice. This may involve research and discernment to learn how he has been operating, in order to discover where he has been hiding, inflicting difficulty and robbing the people of God of our victory.

Only when we bring the enemy to justice can we take back what he has stolen and force him to face the accomplished work of Christ on the cross. We are here to enforce that victory.

Time to Hang Haman's Sons

I mentioned earlier that the Lord awakened me one night to say, *It is time for the hanging of Haman's ten sons.* I knew the story of Esther but did not recall the names of his sons mentioned in

Scripture. When God goes through the trouble of mentioning names, however, they hold special significance.

When Jews read those names, they try to do it all in one breath, indicating that all the sons had been killed and then hanged at the same moment. It represented a complete and utter defeat of the enemy. Esther 9:7–9 lists their names as Parshandatha, Dalphon, Aspatha, Poratha, Adalia, Aridatha, Parmashta, Arisai, Aridai, and Vajezatha. Go ahead and try to read those in one breath!

If it was important enough for the Lord to include the detail of these names in Scripture, and He was telling me prophetically that it was time for them to be hanged, I felt it was important to do some research. How might the meaning of those names contain a demonic assignment to try to continue to rob the people of God? Research could bring insight, enabling us to bring those fugitives before the heavenly court to face their judgment.

When I teach on the meanings of names, I often have people ask me the source of the definitions. Most of the time I use *Strong's Concordance*, Hebrew and Greek lexicons, and a variety of Bible dictionaries (Smith's, Nelson's, and Easton's, to name three). Since Haman's sons' names are Persian, it proved a bit more challenging to discover the exact meaning of their names. So I have added the studies of a few Jewish rabbis to my list of resources, as their search into the significance of the names proved insightful.

One of the interesting things I found is that three of the names (Arisai, Aridai, and Aridatha) are thought to be references to a Persian god named Hari. His name means "one who takes away" or "seizes, plunders, robs; that bears off or removes."[3] This emphasizes the fact that these three sons are descendants of Agag of the Amalekites, the robbers and thieves.

In Hebrew the prefix *ari* refers to a Hebrew word for lion.[4] Lions were symbols of royalty, strength, and the tribe of Judah. But Hebrew scholars also say, "In Biblical times lions symbolized any power (individual or national) that plundered, gathered and hoarded."[5] So even utilizing the Hebrew word assigned to these names reinforces their connection to the idea of plundering.

The Meanings of the Names

Each of the names of Haman's ten sons, I believe, refers to aspects of how the thief attempts to rob God's people. Some of the names may seem to have a positive or virtuous meaning. But when put into the context of robbery, we can suppose those are the very areas the enemy is attempting to steal.

Their names are demonic assignments attempting to lead believers astray. Each name is a demonic decree of death and destruction that must be overthrown. Concerning such decrees, Isaiah 10:1–2 declares:

> Woe to those who decree unrighteous decrees, who write misfortune, which they have prescribed to rob the needy of justice, and to take what is right from the poor of My people, that widows may be their prey, and that they may rob the fatherless.

As we discover the meaning of each name and its decree against God's people, I will suggest a prayer of repentance and a counter-decree, speaking woe to every assignment of evil. I encourage you to speak these out loud.

1. Parshandatha, the Spirit of Distraction

Etymology: In Hebrew this name means "given by prayer."[6] Some Hebrew scholars suggest this name comes from a verb meaning "to expound" and a noun meaning "the law or a decree."[7] Prayer and study of the Law are virtuous things. But Rabbi Mordechai Sasson (1747–1831), a leader in the Jewish community in Baghdad, suggests that this name indicates the enemy's evil strategy to distance a person from the Torah (or Scripture).[8]

Demonic Assignment: The spirit of distraction, leading to apathy, complacency, and spiritual slumber, steals the passion of the believer, keeping us from accomplishing our calling in Christ. It decrees, "You don't have to be so spiritual all the time. Prayer and the Word are nice, but not necessary to live a comfortable life. After all, God is most concerned about your comfort and peace."

This evil tactic causes us to lose our passion for serving Christ. Often as young believers, we cannot get enough of prayer and reading the Word of God. Yet the cares of this world, the lure of entertainment, and the presentation of casual, comfortable Christianity lull us to sleep, causing us to lose sight of our calling and purpose to turn the world upside down.

I once had a dream in which I was driving through neighborhoods shouting out the window, "Wake up! Wake up!" I knew God was saying that much of the Church had fallen asleep and that He wanted to bring another Great Awakening.

Awakening and revival stir the people of God out of spiritual slumber and get us back to our responsibility to change lives with the message of the Gospel. We must wake up and return to prayer, the study of God's Word, worship, and spiritual service.

Prayer of Repentance: Father, forgive me for being led astray by distractions that have separated me from spending time with You. Forgive me for seeking comfort above calling and recreation above relationship. I repent of casual, comfortable Christianity. Stir my passion for You again. Wake me up and restore my first love for Jesus, according to Ephesians 5:14, Revelation 2:4, and Revelation 3:1–2. In Jesus' name I receive freedom and forgiveness. Amen.

A Decree of Victory: I decree woe to the spirit of distraction leading to apathy, complacency, and spiritual slumber. I declare that revival and awakening are breaking out in my life, in my family, and throughout my church and my nation. I take back a passion for prayer, study of the Word, and spiritual service. I activate in myself a fresh love for worship and warfare. I will live a life of purpose and answer God's call on my life from this day forward. Amen.

2. Dalphon, the Religious Spirit

Etymology: In Hebrew the word *dalaph* means to drip or to weep.[9] It can also mean rainmaker[10] or even "house of caves."[11] Caves are a symbol of isolation, hiding, and darkness. Rabbi Mordechai Sasson suggests that this name is associated with *deleth*,[12] the Hebrew word for door, indicating a door to bad intentions, making a person performing a *mitzvah* (good deed or spiritual service) "do so with wrong intentions."[13]

Demonic Assignment: I believe this describes a religious spirit, which 2 Timothy 3:5 says has "a form of godliness but denying its power." It robs believers of authentic relationship with God and cuts them off from the power of the Holy Spirit. It replaces relationship with the true and living God with empty ritual. It replaces the sensitivity toward moves of the Holy Spirit (for example, weeping) with coldness and hardness of heart. It replaces the power of the supernatural through healings, signs, and wonders with doubt, skepticism, reason, and unbelief. The religious spirit decrees, "Your good works will save you. They are enough. You don't need to believe in all that supernatural stuff or even in the Bible. As long as you are good enough, you will get to heaven."

The religious spirit wants us to be rain-seekers, always thinking of ourselves, instead of rainmakers, those called to shift the atmosphere in power. Elijah spoke to the drought and opened the heavens, causing rain to fall on the land. He was a rainmaker.

The religious spirit seeks to keep us in dead religion, performing religious acts (the form) without the reality of the supernatural power of the Holy Spirit in our lives. It wants to trap us in the limitation of our natural minds instead of releasing the spirit part of our being to walk in authority. It wants to keep us in fear rather than letting our faith be fueled.

Jesus told us we would receive "power" (Acts 1:8; Greek, *dunamis*[14]) to do miracles when the Holy Spirit came upon us. We are to be full of the Spirit and walk in faith, authority, and power to fulfill our calling in the earth.

Prayer of Repentance: Father, I repent for every area of my life in which I have allowed a religious spirit to rule. Forgive me for trusting my own mind and heart above Your Word. Forgive me for thinking my works could earn my salvation. Forgive me for living in fear rather than faith. Forgive me for doing good deeds with the wrong heart—to earn my salvation, to look good to others, or to promote myself. I want my relationship with You to be full of faith and power, authentic and real, in Jesus' name. Amen.

A Decree of Victory: I decree woe to the religious spirit that represents a form of godliness but denies God's true power and authority. I decree that I will no longer play church, but I will be God's expression of the Church, His ekklesia, everywhere I go. I am called to rule and reign with Him in the earth. I am called to move in power, releasing signs, wonders, and miracles. I am shifting from a religious mentality that asks, "What's in it for me?" and activating the anointing for me to be a world-changer and rainmaker. I will be a champion of God's move in the earth. I am filled with the Holy Spirit, including His fire and His power. I take back the supernatural power of God in every area of my life. Amen.

3. Aspatha, the Spirit of Mammon

Etymology: In Hebrew this name means "the enticed gathered."[15] Hebrew scholars suggest that this name comes from a verb, *asap*, meaning "to gather or collect, mostly in reference to harvests, and with a connotation of removal." They also suggest the original name in Persian was Aspadata, meaning "given by the horse."[16] In the ancient Persian religion of Zoroastrianism, the horse was considered a gift of wealth.[17] The ending *ta* was a noun meaning chamber or storeroom, which could be a reference to a place where money or valuables are stored. Rabbi Sasson suggests that this refers to a person gathering piles of money to take him away from the study of Torah and doing good deeds.[18]

Demonic Assignment: I believe this is the spirit of mammon (about which I wrote extensively in chapter 5). It does not mean just wealth or money, but it was the ancient Syrian god of wealth and riches. It is an idol that demands worship and threatens to punish all who will not bow down. It is the spirit that steals our prosperity, blessings, and opportunity for increase. It says, "Put your trust in me rather than God. Don't worry about wasting your money paying tithes or giving offerings. Money answers everything." Those who align with mammon's way of thinking in attitude or action forfeit any position of blessing, prosperity, or increase from the Lord.

It is for this reason that Scripture warns us that "the love of money is the root of all evil" (1 Timothy 6:10 KJV). God loves to bless His people, but this demonic assignment wants to hold believers in lack or poverty and lock up their ability to move forward with the call of God, or else to corrupt their purpose through wrongful pursuit of money, getting their priorities out of alignment.

The enemy always tries to lock up resources by shutting up the heavenly storehouse. God tells us in Malachi 3 that when we bring our tithes and offerings into the earthly storehouse, He opens up the heavenly one and pours out blessings so abundant we will not have room enough to receive them.

Prayer of Repentance: Father, I repent for every time I have agreed and aligned myself with the spirit of mammon. I ask You to forgive me for every ungodly mentality regarding my financial supply—for mentalities of lack, poverty, and scarcity, as well as greed, avarice, and materialism. Forgive me for the times I have disobeyed You because I was afraid of how much it would cost. Forgive me for not trusting You to supply my every need. In Jesus' name. Amen.

A Decree of Victory: I decree woe to the spirit of mammon, including strongholds of poverty, lack, scarcity, greed, avarice, materialism, and fear. I decree that I will seek first God's Kingdom and His righteousness, and then everything else will be added unto me. My Father owns the cattle on a thousand hills, so I will put my trust in Him only. I decree that God is opening His storehouse of blessing over my life and releasing opportunities, promotions, and increase in every area. I am blessed and not cursed because I serve the true and living God. Amen.

4. Poratha, a Spirit of Seduction and Perversion

Etymology: In Hebrew this name means either fruitfulness or frustration.[19] Rabbi Sasson says this word spelled backward in the Talmud indicates a woman's private parts. This evil, he says, causes one to want to look at uncovered women.[20]

Demonic Assignment: I believe that this is a spirit of seduction and sexual perversion. Freedom from this spirit produces a fruitful life, whereas bondage leads to a life of frustration.

Revelation 2:20 speaks of a woman named Jezebel in the first-century church in Thyatira who was allowed "to teach and seduce My servants to commit sexual immorality." Queen Jezebel from the Old Testament personifies this spirit. The word *seduce* in this passage means to deceive or lead astray,[21] and the phrase *to commit sexual immorality* in the same passage is the Greek *porneusai*, from which we get the word *pornography*. It means to act the harlot, to indulge unlawful lust,[22] to give oneself to unlawful sexual intercourse.[23] The spirit of Jezebel uses sexual perversion to control individuals and keep them from their destiny. It destroys churches and families. Many leaders have fallen prey to this destructive spirit.

This spirit decrees, "You were made for pleasure. Who are you hurting to indulge in viewing pornography or participating in illicit sexual behavior? Between consenting adults, it's fine. You should follow your desires and not feel guilty. That's just the thinking of a repressed society."

This spirit steals personal purity and innocence and leads to shame and condemnation. It robs marriages, families, and children. It often causes divorce. Never believe that this is a victimless sin.

Prayer of Repentance: Father, I repent for anytime I have given place to seduction, sexual perversion, lust, or wrong behavior. Forgive me for anytime I have viewed nudity through any form of media or participated in an illicit sexual experience. I realize this is wrong. It is a sin against You, my own purity, and my family. Forgive me for allowing my heart to be stirred with lust.

I ask You to wash me and make me clean through the blood of Jesus. I don't want to live a frustrated, fruitless life, but to follow You in every way. In Jesus' mighty name I pray.

A Decree of Victory: I decree woe to every assignment of sexual perversion, seduction, and Jezebel. I will not be controlled by illicit and ungodly sexual behavior. I will keep my eyes on the Lord and not on things that stir lust. I will walk free from every addictive behavior that seeks to keep me in bondage. I take back my purity and innocence by the power of the cross. I take back wholeness in my marriage and/or family. I break every generational curse off my children and declare, "As for me and my house, we will serve the LORD" (Joshua 24:15).

5. Adalia, the Spirit of Pride and Rebellion

Etymology: In Old Persian and Hebrew, this name means "I shall be drawn up of Jah"[24]—which may not suggest a lot to modern readers. But Rabbi Sasson comments that it comes from a word meaning "lifted up," implying haughtiness and arrogance.[25] The name can also mean brave or strong in mind, or fire god.[26]

Demonic Assignment: In drawing on Rabbi Sasson's definition of "lifted up with haughtiness and arrogance," we can see where the aspect of being strong-minded comes in. God desires that we have strong minds submitted to Him. But if our minds become strong and stubborn against Him, we are in trouble. Proverbs 16:18 warns us, "Pride goes before destruction, and a haughty spirit before a fall." James 4:6 declares, "God resists the proud, but gives grace to the humble." Pride, self-sufficiency, independence, haughtiness, and arrogance are always the enemy's trap.

This enemy declares, "You can do it yourself. Go your own way. You don't need God to help you. You are as strong and smart as God." It was prideful thinking that caused the fall of Lucifer.

This is a spirit of false governance, usurping authority from legitimate leaders. This kind of thinking has shipwrecked many believers on their path to purpose, and compromised the callings of many great men and women of God. It steals humility and thwarts destiny, even the destinies of nations that reject God.

This spirit may be related to Leviathan, a creature depicted in nature as a sea serpent or crocodile. In Job 41:34 he is called "king over all the children of pride." He looks like an undefeatable foe. But Psalm 74:14 states that God will destroy this many-headed monster, with his twisted communications and ungodly spells, and He will break in pieces his many heads.

Prayer of Repentance: Father, I come to You humbly, in full repentance for the pride in my life. Forgive me for thinking I don't need You. Forgive me for foolish independence and haughty self-reliance. I need You in every area of my life. Forgive me for the times I have resisted the Holy Spirit's dealings in my heart. I repent and humble myself under Your mighty hand, knowing You will raise me up in due time. I submit myself to You, knowing from James 4:7 that if I resist the devil, he will flee.

I join my prayers with those of other humble believers, repenting for the sins of my nation—for our pride and stubbornness in refusing to follow Your ways. I pray that as we humble ourselves, You will show grace and heal our land.

A Decree of Victory: I decree woe to the spirits of pride, haughtiness, and arrogance that have tried to invade my heart and mind. I decree my dependence on You, Lord, and break every Luciferian assignment off my life that tries to lure me into self-exaltation and independence, and every spirit of Leviathan that traps me in self-focus. I will be strong in the Lord and in the power of His might, but I will remain humble, teachable, and sensitive to the Holy Spirit. I reclaim my leadership calling and my destiny in Christ.

I decree woe to every Luciferian spirit and Leviathan's crooked, twisted way in government. Your resistance to God's ways will be exposed and broken into pieces. The Lord has put a hook in your jaw and will expose all your backroom deals, crooked connections, lies, and deceit in my land. Crooked places are being made straight, in Jesus' name.

6. Aridatha, the Voice of Accusation and Oppression

Etymology: In Hebrew this word means "lion of the decree."[27] In Persian it might be related to the phrase *given by Hari*.[28] Remember that Hari was a Persian god whose name meant to plunder, to seize, or to take away. The lion was also a symbol of plundering, gathering, or hoarding by governments or individuals.

Demonic Assignment: Clearly this name indicates the activity of the thief. But how and what specifically is being stolen? I believe this name speaks of the unrighteous decrees of the enemy that are filling our airwaves. We are being bombarded constantly by ungodly ideologies through media, music, and messages. These demonic broadcasts are part of the voice war raging in the earth today as this enemy seeks to control the narrative. The voice of the enemy has been unleashed to drown out the voice of truth, the voice of the Lord. This is a spirit of oppression, accusation, and besiegement.

I once had a dream about an attack coming from one known as Rabshakeh. He was trying to poison a righteous leader and break him. When I woke up, I found that Rabshakeh was either the name or the title of the negotiator for Sennacherib, king of Assyria, when he besieged Jerusalem in 2 Kings 18 and

217

Isaiah 36. He filled the atmosphere with lies and bombarded the people with threats in order to get them to give up in fear. This is the nature of this spirit. It wants to rob us of our determination and ability to stand fast and not quit. It wants to take our spiritual strength.

It says, "Just give up. You can't beat me. You don't have the strength or the resources to stand through this fight. You are weak and defeated. You can't even hear the voice of the Lord. You might as well just quit and give in to me. I've got you surrounded." The real danger comes when we believe what he says and even speak it with our own mouths, agreeing with our mortal enemy.

Prayer of Repentance: Father, forgive me for listening to the voice of the enemy. I repent of hearing his voice louder than Your voice. I repent for feeling weak and defeated when You said I am filled with Your supernatural power. Give me ears to hear all You are saying. Let Your Word fill my heart, mind, and mouth. Forgive me for speaking words of defeat, empowering the oppressor and accuser over my life. I will say what You say instead, in Jesus' mighty name.

A Decree of Victory: I say woe to every spirit of accusation, oppression, and besiegement, and declare my freedom in Christ. I know from Isaiah 30:31 that the voice of the Lord is far more powerful and shatters the enemy. Rather than the robber being the lion of the decree, I am the lion of the decree, and I am filling the atmosphere with praise, breaking the spirit of heaviness and releasing freedom, joy, and celebration in Christ. I will roar with the voice of the Lord. I will not give up! I will not quit! I will press the battle to the full. My enemy will be ensnared with the words of his own mouth. His curses are boomeranging back on his own head. I am victorious through Christ Jesus. Amen.

7. Parmashta, the Antichrist *Spirit of Division*

Etymology: In Hebrew this word means "superior."[29] Rabbi Sasson says the name refers to that which rips apart the strong connection between fellow Jews.[30]

Demonic Assignment: This is a spirit of division that steals the unity among believers. It stirs up strife, hatred, and contention in families, marriages, and relationships, causing separation, isolation, and devastation. It is fueled by unrighteous ideologies and the "woke" agenda that erodes common sense and biblical foundations through its sense of superiority. The divisiveness of cancel culture declares, "Unless you agree with me, I will cut you off. In fact, I will publicly shame you for your archaic biblical worldview, and make sure you lose relationships, friendships, and even jobs and opportunities."

This spirit of division is politically motivated to divide and conquer. It is rooted in an antichrist spirit (again, meaning *against Christ*). It wants to destroy churches through breaking down boundaries of morality and compromising biblical truth. It seeks to destroy the nuclear family, redefining marriage and sexuality, and indoctrinating children to separate them from parental guidance.

Prayer of Repentance: Father, I repent of every area in which I have allowed division to rule me. Forgive me for giving place to strife, hatred, and contention and for not walking in daily forgiveness toward those who offend me. Forgive me for any way I have aligned with the antichrist spirit, the woke agenda, and cancel culture. Instead of being woke, I pray for an awakening. Forgive me for passivity when the enemy has been advancing in my land. Open my eyes to every tactic of the enemy so I can push back the gates of hell. In Jesus' powerful name. Amen.

A Decree of Victory: I decree woe to every spirit of division, strife, and contention in Jesus' name. Where there is unity, God commands the blessing, so I take back unity in my family, my marriage, my church, my business, and my community. I break every antichrist assignment to divide and conquer. I decree scales are falling off the eyes of those who have been deceived by woke ideology. I take back the schools in my community— from daycare through college—and drive deceptive spirits out. Rather than being woke, let a new awakened generation arise in our land and walk in generational unity, for it is there that God commands the blessing.

8. Arisai, the Spirit of Witchcraft and Occult Powers

Etymology: In Hebrew *Arisai* means lion-like.[31] This is another of the names of Haman's sons rooted in the name of the Persian god Ari (or Hari), the god of plunder. Once again we have a reference to the lion and to Hari. How does this spirit plunder and rob? Rabbi Sasson believes the name means that "it continuously poisons a person with the venom of the snake."[32]

Demonic Assignment: In Scripture the snake is a symbol of pure evil, the devil himself. He appeared in the Garden in the form of a serpent to tempt Eve. The snake injects poison into its prey, bringing paralysis and death. The Hebrew word *serpent* comes from a root word that means to hiss, to whisper a magic spell, to prognosticate,[33] or related to the practice of divination.[34] This spirit tries to rob believers of victory.

The enemy seeks to trap unsuspecting, unlearned, carnal believers in occult practices such as reading tarot cards, playing with Ouiji boards, reading horoscopes, and watching occult programming on television or in movies—practices that are seemingly harmless. These practices are *not* harmless. And there is much of it on the airwaves today—a blatant glorifi-

220

cation of evil drawing many in. The younger generation in particular is being targeted by fascination with dark powers.

Those practicing witchcraft release spells on individuals, churches, and even nations, attempting to bring them into bondage. While witchcraft is the voice of evil, true prophetic people must arise to break divination by the prophetic voice of the Lord.

Prayer of Repentance: Father, I repent for any open door through which I have allowed the spirit of witchcraft to enter. Your Word says rebellion is as the sin of witchcraft, so I repent of any rebellion in my heart or actions. I repent of participating in any occult practices or viewing occult programming on any form of media. I ask You, Lord, to cleanse my eye gate, ear gate, and heart gate of anything I have seen, heard, or done. In the name above all names, Jesus, and by the power of His shed blood. Amen.

A Decree of Victory: I decree woe to every spirit of witchcraft and every occult power aligned against me. I declare according to Isaiah 54:17 that no weapon formed against me will prosper and every tongue that rises up against me in judgment I condemn. I decree that every hex or curse sent against me to do me harm will come to nothing, for I am covered by the blood of Jesus. I decree that every curse will be turned to a blessing because God loves me. I decree that light will shine in the darkness and drive it out. I take back my victory over evil.

I decree that God's prophetic people are arising and will prophesy with accuracy and power. The true voice of God will break the power of every false word, divination, and prognostication. I will prophesy and demons will flee, in Jesus' name. Amen.

9. Aridai, the Spirits of Fear, Worry, Anxiety, and Intimidation

Etymology: In Hebrew *Aridai* means "the lion is enough."[35] In Persian it may mean "delight of Hari."[36] (Once again the lion and Hari speak of plundering.) Rabbi Sasson says this name refers to "the evil that subjugates a righteous person with suffering and worries about his livelihood."[37]

Demonic Assignment: This is a spirit of fear with its accompanying spirits of worry, anxiety, and intimidation. First John 4:18 tells us that "fear involves torment." It will shut you up and shut you down. It steals courage and creativity. If the enemy paralyzes you with fear, you will not advance. This spirit says, "Play it safe. Remain stuck in your dead-end job because, after all, it's safer. You don't want to be bold in Christ; you might fail. You don't want to step out of your comfort zone. Don't try to use your gifts; it may not work out."

I hate the spirit of fear. As I have said, it was one of the greatest strongholds over my life. I found that a vain (and overactive) imagination often prophesied fearsome outcomes to me about my life and family. Yes, the devil prophesies, too! Goliath prophesied to David that his body would be fed to the birds of the air. David, rather than entertain that fearsome outcome, prophesied right back to the giant of his own demise—and *that* prophecy came true. We must come out of agreement with and stop giving place to the spirits of fear, worry, and intimidation. Only then can we live out our prophetic destinies.

Prayer of Repentance: Father, I recognize that whatever is not of faith is sin. Therefore, I repent of every area of my life in which I have partnered with the spirit of fear. Forgive me for failing to take my thoughts captive and make them obedient to Christ. Forgive me for allowing vain imaginations to prophesy death and destruction over my life and for the anxiety they produced. I cancel every lie and worry that has held me in bondage, and I repent for giving place to the torment of fear. Thank You for setting me free, in Jesus' name.

A Decree of Victory: I decree woe to every spirit of fear, worry, anxiety, and intimidation. I break the power these spirits have held over my life. I take back courage. I take back boldness. I take back the spirit of adventure. I take back the anointing for exploration. I activate the anointing for creativity and entrepreneurship. I stir up my spiritual gifts and will not be held back by the spirit of fear, since I have been given power, love, and a sound mind, full of self-control. I will move in signs, wonders, and miracles because I am free. In Jesus' name. Amen.

10. Vajezatha, a Spirit of Prejudice

Etymology: In Hebrew *Vajezatha* may mean strong like the wind[38] or "son of the atmosphere."[39] The concept of atmosphere speaks of that which surrounds us at all times. It may also refer to the spiritual or cultural atmosphere in which we live. Rabbi Sasson says this name means "the bitterness of the olive, symbolizing bitter and strong judgement."[40]

Demonic Assignment: This name indicates a spirit of prejudice rooted in bitterness, hatred, and victimhood, creating a negative—and at times demon-filled—atmosphere over a nation. Prejudice causes people to prejudge others out of their own unhealthy experience, ideology, or bitterness. It causes them to devalue or disrespect who God has created others to be. This can be racial prejudice (racism), including antisemitism (against Jewish people) and others' external appearance or the color of their skin. It can be socioeconomic prejudice, judging others for their social or economic status, whether rich or poor. It can be based on gender, prejudging people's value based on their being male or female. It steals justice and opportunity from those judged. It steals dignity. It steals blessings. It is evil. It is exactly what Haman expressed toward the Jewish people.

This spirit says, "These individuals are not worthy of your trust or respect because they are less than you. They don't look or act like you. They are different, and undeserving of dignity." God hates this attitude and when His people give place to it in their lives.

Prayer of Repentance: Father, forgive me for every time I have prejudged others based on the color of their skin, their gender, their education level, or how much money they may or may not have. Forgive me for not recognizing the image of God in each person and for rejecting and disrespecting sinners, failing to share Your love.

Since this is often a subconscious judgment, please open my eyes to whenever I am not treating others fairly, when I am dis-respecting them or robbing them of their dignity. I realize this breaks Your heart. Please forgive me and make me sensitive to the needs of others. And forgive me for carrying bitterness from the times I have been the victim of someone else's prejudice. I forgive the persons who offended or judged me, and I release them from all judgment. In Jesus' name.

A Decree of Victory: I decree woe to the spirits of prejudice, racism, antisemitism, bitterness, and hatred, and declare that these have no part in my life. I will honor the image of God in each person and be respectful to those who are not like me. Even when I perceive that they are sinners, I decree that I will shine the love of Jesus to them and share the good news of His saving grace with kindness and respect. I take back true justice, wisdom, life, and truth. I take back dignity and blessings.

I decree that the Church, the ekklesia, *will get right what culture has gotten wrong. We will be a multicultural body living in unity and respect, called to change the atmosphere of the world in which we live. Let Your Kingdom come, Father, and Your will be done on earth as it is in the atmosphere of heaven.*

ACTIVATION

Whew! I know this study of all those names was a lot! But I hope you see how each of the names of Haman's ten sons corresponds to an area the enemy has tried to steal from us. We are empowered in the name of Jesus to take back seven times what was stolen!

Now is the time to make a list of everything you have realized has been stolen from you by the enemy. Focus on two or three of the above areas and write your own decree to speak out loud. Use Scriptures in writing your decree. Then, with authority, begin to decree and command a taking back of all that was stolen and divine recovery in every area of your life and family.

QUESTIONS TO CONSIDER

1. Do you see evidence of any of the above "sons of Haman" operating in your own life or family?
2. How do you feel this has affected or limited your spiritual journey?
3. What habits, mindsets, or ungodly beliefs do you need to change in order to experience victory in your life?
4. Do you recognize any area in which the enemy has stolen from you, due to the above responses? Write a decree to take it back.

FINAL CHARGE

I pray that the Lord has opened your eyes to the tactics and devices of the thief in your life and that you have a new determination to confront him. No more "this is just life" mentality. No more passivity. No more sense of helplessness or hopelessness. No more fear or regret. I pray that you have been empowered to rise up and take back all he has stolen, and to decree divine recovery over your own heart, family, and life.

Jesus died and paid a price for us to experience abundant life. That does not mean our lives will constantly be easy, but rather that we have been empowered by the Holy Spirit to recover everything necessary to fulfill God's divine call upon our lives.

Walking out our faith can at times feel like a battle. It is for this reason that God is issuing a call to arms to His people, to show up for the battle and to engage the enemy, using our spiritual weapons to advance His Kingdom against all encroaching darkness and to enforce the victory Christ won at the cross. Jude 1:3 in *The Message* exhorts us:

> Dear friends, I've dropped everything to write you about this life of salvation that we have in common. I have to write

insisting—begging!—that you fight with everything you have in you for this faith entrusted to us as a gift to guard and cherish.

Will you answer God's call to arms?

God's Promise of Recovery

Zechariah 9:11–12 in *The Amplified Bible, Classic Edition* tells us of God's promise of double-portion restoration, regardless of the pit we have found ourselves in:

> As for you also, because of and for the sake of the [covenant of the Lord with His people, which was sealed with sprinkled] covenant blood, I have released and sent forth your imprisoned people out of the waterless pit. Return to the stronghold [of security and prosperity], you prisoners of hope; even today do I declare that I will restore double your former prosperity to you.

The Message says it this way:

> And you, because of my blood covenant with you, I'll release your prisoners from their hopeless cells. Come home, hope–filled prisoners! This very day I'm declaring a double bonus—everything you lost returned twice-over!

You may have been robbed. You may have been through it. You may have fought battles you feel you have lost. You may have been taken captive. But God is releasing you from captivity and restoring all to you, a promised double for your trouble.

In Joel 3:1 God says, "For behold, in those days and at that time when I shall reverse the captivity and restore the fortunes of Judah and Jerusalem" (AMPC). I like to read it, "In these days and at this time." God is the God of restoration, freedom, and a mighty comeback.

A FINAL DECREE OF VICTORY

I want to release one more decree for you to speak out loud to proclaim your victory.

I decree that the time for the hanging of Haman's sons has come. Enough is enough of the enemy's strategies to rob the people of God, and even nations, of their destinies. I repent for any place I have partnered with their evil plots. I repent of any lie I have believed or any place I have yielded to the enemy in my life. Deliver me from evil, Lord, by the name and power of the blood of Jesus.

I decree that the Esther Church, the ekklesia, *is rising in power, in truth, and in new authority, and I answer the call to arms. The scepter of favor has been extended to me. I can write new decrees that bring divine reversal. It is a time of turnaround, a boomerang season, when everything the enemy meant against me and my family for evil is turned for our good. It is a time of revival for me, my family, and my land. I decree that an awakening has begun.*

It is a season of joy. It is my time to rise up and take back all that the enemy has stolen, in Jesus' name. He may have come against me one way, but he will flee seven ways. He may have stolen from me, but he has to give back seven times what he stole. I decree divine recovery over my life and family. In Jesus' name. Amen.

NOTES

Introduction

1. *Britannica*, s.v. "Ecclesia," accessed September 21, 2023, https://www.britannica.com/topic/Ecclesia-ancient-Greek-assembly.

2. Jane Hamon, *Discernment: The Essential Guide to Hearing the Voice of God* (Minneapolis: Chosen, 2019), 25–27.

3. Jane Hamon, *Declarations for Breakthrough: Agreeing with the Voice of God* (Minneapolis: Chosen, 2021), 163–164.

4. Nilda Tsounis, "Amalek, the Enemy of Israel," Yahshua Ha Masiaj, October 1, 2014, http://yahshuaeselmashiaj.blogspot.com/2014/10/amalek-enemy-of-israel.html.

5. Arnold Slyper, "Who was Amalek?," Bible-pedia.org, accessed September 21, 2023, http://bible-pedia.org/amalek.

6. James Strong, *Strong's Exhaustive Concordance of the Bible* (McLean, Va.: MacDonald Publishing, 1980), Hebrew 8154.

7. Strong, Hebrew 8555, 4513.

8. Strong, Hebrew 464.

Chapter 1 Divine Recovery

1. James Strong, *Strong's Exhaustive Concordance of the Bible* (McLean, Va.: MacDonald Publishing, 1980), Greek 4053.

2. Joseph Henry Thayer, *Thayer's Greek-English Lexicon of the New Testament* (Grand Rapids: Baker, 1987), 4053.

3. *American Heritage® Dictionary of the English Language*, fifth edition, s.v. "recover" (New York: HarperCollins, 2022), https://www.ahdictionary.com/word/search.html?q=recover&submit.x=0&submit.y=0.

4. Charlton Laird, *Webster's New World Thesaurus*, s.v. "recovery" (New York: Warner Books, 1982).

5. "Take Back Your Property through Replevin," Community Legal Services, June 22, 2021, https://www.clsmf.org/take-back-your-property-through-replevin/.

6. Strong, Greek 3875.

7. Thayer, 3875.

8. Strong, Greek 3954.

9. Thayer, 3954.

10. Strong, Greek 1656.

11. Thayer, 1656.

12. Rick Renner, *Sparkling Gems from the Greek*, vol. 2 (Shippensburg, Pa.: Harrison House, 2017), 690.

13. Thayer, 1656.

14. "Appeal to Heaven—History," An Appeal to Heaven, accessed September 25, 2023, https://www.appealtoheaven.org/#heaven.

15. Dave Benner, "John Locke's Appeal to Heaven: Its Continuing Relevance," Tenth Amendment Center, April 16, 2017, https://tenthamendmentcenter.com/2017/04/16/john-lockes-appeal-to-heaven-its-continuing-relevance/.

16. Strong, Hebrew 7725.

17. Robert Gay, *Voices: Hearing and Discerning When God Speaks* (Melbourne, Fl.: Parsons, 2021), 148–150.

Chapter 2 Possessing Our Promise

1. Joseph Henry Thayer, *Thayer's Greek-English Lexicon of the New Testament* (Grand Rapids: Baker, 1987), 4053.

2. Rhema Team, "The God Who Is More Than Enough," Kenneth Hagin Ministries, June 8, 2020, https://events.rhema.org/the-god-who-is-more-than-enough/.

3. James Strong, *Strong's Exhaustive Concordance of the Bible* (McLean, Va.: MacDonald Publishing, 1980), Hebrew 669.

4. Francis Brown, S. R. Driver, and Charles A. Briggs, *The Brown-Driver-Briggs Hebrew and English Lexicon* (Peabody, Mass.: Hendrickson, 20th printing, 2021), 3063.

Chapter 3 Taking Back Our Peace

1. James Strong, *Strong's Exhaustive Concordance of the Bible* (McLean, Va.: MacDonald Publishing, 1980), Greek 1515.

2. Joseph Henry Thayer, *Thayer's Greek-English Lexicon of the New Testament* (Grand Rapids: Baker, 1987), 515.

3. Strong, Hebrew 8269.

4. Strong, Hebrew 8323.

5. Strong, Hebrew 7965.

6. Christian Cerdan, "The Disruptive Power of Shalom," Christian Cerdan blog, December 15, 2021, https://christiancerdan.com/blog/2021/12/15/the-disruptive-power-of-shalom/.

7. William Smith, *Smith's Bible Dictionary* (Grand Rapids: Zondervan, 1974), 951b.

8. Francis Frangipane, *The Three Battlegrounds: An In-Depth View of the Three Arenas of Spiritual Warfare: The Mind, the Church and the Heavenly Places* (Marion, Oh.: Advancing Church Publications, 1989), 1.

9. Joyce Meyer, *Battlefield of the Mind: Winning the Battle in Your Mind* (Fenton, Mo.: FaithWords, Fenton, Mo., 2011), 3.

10. Strong, Greek 5432.

11. Thayer, 5432.

12. Thayer, 2588.

13. Strong, Greek 3540.

14. Brett Lee, "Stayin' Alive: That's What Friends Are For," *BYU News*, July 26, 2010, https://news.byu.edu/news/stayin-alive-thats-what-friends-are.

15. Stephen Ilardi, "Social Isolation: A Modern Plague," *Psychology Today*, July 13, 2009, https://www.psychologytoday.com/us/blog/the-depression-cure/200907/social-isolation-a-modern-plague.

16. Strong, Hebrew 3581.

17. J. Sidlow Baxter, *Awake, My Heart* (Grand Rapids: Zondervan, 1960), 10.

18. Strong, Hebrew 5749.

19. Francis Brown, S. R. Driver, and Charles A. Briggs, *The Brown-Driver-Briggs Hebrew and English Lexicon* (Peabody, Mass.: Hendrickson, 20th printing, 2021), 5749.

Chapter 4 Taking Back Our Prosperity

1. Dictionary.com, s.v. "prosperity," accessed November 2, 2023, https://www.dictionary.com/browse/prosperity.

2. James Strong, *Strong's Exhaustive Concordance of the Bible* (McLean, Va.: MacDonald Publishing, 1980), Hebrew 6743.

3. Francis Brown, S. R. Driver, and Charles A. Briggs, *The Brown-Driver-Briggs Hebrew and English Lexicon* (Peabody, Mass.: Hendrickson, 20th printing, 2021), 6743.

4. Strong, Greek 2137.

5. Strong, Hebrew 4080, 4079.

6. Strong, Hebrew 1809.

7. Cambridge Dictionary, s.v. "courage," accessed October 24, 2023, https://dictionary.cambridge.org/us/dictionary/english/courage.

8. Strong, Greek 165.

9. Strong, Greek 2416, 2417.

Chapter 5 Prosperity Principles

1. *Collins Dictionary*, s.v. "revive," accessed October 24, 2023, https://www.collinsdictionary.com/us/dictionary/english/revive.

2. *Merriam-Webster Dictionary*, s.v. "pro," accessed October 24, 2023, https://www.merriam-webster.com/dictionary/pro.

3. *Merriam-Webster Dictionary*, s.v. "provision," accessed October 24, 2023, https://www.merriam-webster.com/dictionary/provision.

4. James Strong, *Strong's Exhaustive Concordance of the Bible* (McLean, Va.: MacDonald Publishing, 1980), Hebrew 6213.

5. Strong, Greek 4147.

6. Thayer, 4147.

7. Anne Kamaya, "Mammon History, Biblical Significance & References," Study.com, February 25, 2023, https://study.com/academy/lesson/mammon-origin-history-bible.html.

8. Os Hillman, "God versus Mammon," *Today God Is First*, August 1, 2023, https://todaygodisfirst.com/god-versus-mammon/.

9. Jimmy Evans, quoted in Robert Morris, "Breaking the Spirit of Mammon," *The Blessed Life*, Gateway Devotions, accessed November 2, 2023, https://gatewaydevotions.com/blessedlife/11/.

Chapter 6 Taking Back Our Purpose

1. James Strong, *Strong's Exhaustive Concordance of the Bible* (McLean, Va.: MacDonald Publishing, 1980), Hebrew 6428.

2. Ryan Nelson, "Who Was John Mark?," OverviewBible, April 17, 2019, https://overviewbible.com/john-mark/.

3. *American Heritage Dictionary*, s.v. "comeback," accessed October 30, 2023, https://ahdictionary.com/word/search.html?q=comeback&submit.x=24&submit.y=19.

4. *The Britannica Dictionary*, s.v. "comeback," accessed October 30, 2023, https://www.britannica.com/dictionary/comeback.

5. Strong, Hebrew 3002, 3001.

6. Strong, Hebrew 7307.

7. Francis Brown, S. R. Driver, and Charles A. Briggs, *The Brown-Driver-Briggs Hebrew and English Lexicon* (Peabody, Mass.: Hendrickson, 20th printing, 2021), 924–926.

Chapter 7 Taking Back Our Posterity

1. Cheryl Sacks, *Fire on the Family Altar: Experience the Holy Spirit's Power in Your Home* (Shippensburg, Pa.: Destiny Image, 2023), 7.

2. Dictionary.com, s.v. "posterity," accessed November 2, 2023, https://www.dictionary.com/browse/posterity.

3. Edward Kruk, "Father Absence, Father Deficit, Father Hunger," *Psychology Today*, May 23, 2012, http://www.psychologytoday.com/blog/co-parenting-after-divorce/201205/father-absence-father-deficit-father-hunger.

4. "The Statistics Don't Lie: Fathers Matter," National Fatherhood Initiative, based on data from the U.S. Census Bureau, 2022, https://www.fatherhood.org/father-absence-statistic.

5. Stephen Mansfield, *Never Give In: The Extraordinary Character of Winston Churchill* (Nashville: Cumberland House, 1995), 190.

6. Dr. Sandie Freed, *Warfare Strategies for Kingdom Advancement: Discerning the Absalom Spirit and Roots of the Fatherless Generations* (Tustin, Calif.: Trilogy Christian Publishing, 2023), 206.

7. Rochester Area Fatherhood Network, "Engaged Dads, Strong Families, Enriched Communities," Research and Statistics, accessed November 3, 2023, http://www.rochesterareafatherhoodnetwork.org/statistics#.

8. Online Etymology Dictionary, s.v. "discourage," accessed November 2, 2023, https://www.etymonline.com/search?q=discourage.

9. Online Etymology Dictionary, s.v. "encourage," accessed November 2, 2023, https://www.etymonline.com/word/encourage.

10. Dennis Peacocke, *Doing Business God's Way* (Santa Rosa, Calif.: Rebuild, 1995), 33, 35, 38.

Chapter 8 Taking Back Our Health

1. *Collins Dictionary*, s.v. "feeble," accessed November 9, 2023, https://www.collinsdictionary.com/us/dictionary/english/feeble.

2. Joseph Henry Thayer, *Thayer's Greek-English Lexicon of the New Testament* (Grand Rapids: Baker, 1987), 5375.

3. James Strong, *Strong's Exhaustive Concordance of the Bible* (McLean, Va.: MacDonald Publishing, 1980), Hebrew 2483, 2470.

4. Strong, Hebrew 4341.

5. Strong, Hebrew 6588.

6. Strong, Hebrew 5771.

7. Thayer, 5771.

8. Strong, Hebrew 7965.

9. Thayer, 7965.

10. Strong, Hebrew 7495.

11. Strong, Greek 3900.

12. Strong, Greek 769.

13. Rick Renner, *Sparkling Gems from the Greek*, vol. 2 (Shippensburg, Pa.: Harrison House, 2017), 911.

14. Strong, Greek 4982.

15. Thayer, 4982.

16. See Proverbs 18:20–21; 3 John 2; Isaiah 53:4–5; 1 Peter 2:24; Leviticus 17:11; 1 John 3:8; Psalm 118:17; Galatians 2:20; John 10:10; Romans 8:11; 1 Corinthians 6:19–20; Ephesians 3:19; Isaiah 58:8; Proverbs 17:22; Psalm 103:2–3; Proverbs 4:22.

Chapter 9 Taking Back Our Passion

1. "Haman's Genocidal Plot," The Bible Commentary, accessed November 30, 2023, https://bible.ucg.org/bible-commentary/Esther/Haman's-plot-against-the-Jews/.

2. James Strong, *Strong's Exhaustive Concordance of the Bible* (McLean, Va.: MacDonald Publishing, 1980), Hebrew 7812.

3. Strong, Greek 69.

4. Joseph Henry Thayer, *Thayer's Greek-English Lexicon of the New Testament* (Grand Rapids: Baker, 1987), 69.

5. Wordnik, s.v. "intercede," accessed December 1, 2023, https://www.wordnik.com/words/intercede.

6. James Strong, *Strong's Exhaustive Concordance of the Bible* (McLean, Va.: MacDonald Publishing, 1980), Greek 2729.

Chapter 10 The Hanging of Haman's Ten Sons

1. Cnaan Liphshiz, "Hitler as Haman? An Amsterdam Museum Holds a Relic of That Post-Holocaust Purim Tradition," Jewish Telegraphic Agency, February 25, 2021, https://www.jta.org/2021/02/25/global/hitler-as-haman-an-amsterdam-museum-holds-a-relic-of-that-post-holocaust-purim-tradition.

2. Indeed Editorial Team, "How to Become a Fugitive Recovery Agent in 8 Steps," Indeed Career Guide, updated June 30, 2023, https://www.indeed.com/career-advice/finding-a-job/how-to-become-fugitive-recovery-agent.

3. Gabe Hiemstra, Wisdom Library, s.v. "Hari," accessed December 5, 2023, https://www.wisdomlib.org/definition/hari.

4. James Strong, *Strong's Exhaustive Concordance of the Bible* (McLean, Va.: MacDonald Publishing, 1980), Hebrew 738.

5. "Arioch meaning," Abarim Publications, accessed December 5, 2023, https://www.abarim-publications.com/Meaning/Arioch.html.

6. William Smith, *Smith's Bible Dictionary* (Grand Rapids: Zondervan, 1974), 482.

7. "Parshandatha meaning," Abarim Publications, accessed December 5, 2023, https://www.abarim-publications.com/Meaning/Parshandatha.html.

8. Mi Yodeya, "What Meaning Do the Names of the Ten Sons of Haman Have?," Stack Exchange, accessed December 5, 2023, https://judaism.stackexchange.com/questions/28326/what-meaning-do-the-names-of-the-ten-sons-of-haman-have.

9. Strong, Hebrew 1813, 1811.

10. "Dalphon meaning," Abarim Publications, accessed December 8, 2023, https://www.abarim-publications.com/Meaning/Dalphon.html.

11. *Hitchcock's Bible Names*, s.v. "Dalphon," BibleTools.org, https://www.bibletools.org/index.cfm/fuseaction/Def.show/RTD/Hitchcock/ID/625/Dalphon.htm.

12. Strong, Hebrew 1817.

13. Yodeya, "What Meaning Do the Names . . . ?"

14. Strong, Greek 1411.

15. Francis Brown, S. R. Driver, and Charles A. Briggs, *The Brown-Driver-Briggs Hebrew and English Lexicon* (Peabody, Mass.: Hendrickson, 20th printing, 2021), 630.

16. "Aspatha meaning," Abarim Publications, accessed December 5, 2023, https://www.abarim-publications.com/Meaning/Aspatha.html.

17. Ramiyar Karanjia, "What Is the Status of a Horse in Zoroastrian Religion?," September 7, 2018, https://ramiyarkaranjia.com/2018/09/07/what-is-the-status-of-a-horse-in-zoroastrian-religion-tmy-jj-of-8-7-15-7-22-7-and-29-7-18/.

18. Yodeya, "What Meaning Do the Names . . . ?"

19. QuotesCosmos, s.v. "poratha," accessed December 14, 2023, https://www.quotescosmos.com/bible/bible-concordance/H6334.html.

20. Yodeya, "What Meaning Do the Names . . . ?"

21. Strong, Greek 4105.

22. Strong, Greek 4203.

23. Joseph Henry Thayer, *Thayer's Greek-English Lexicon of the New Testament* (Grand Rapids: Baker, 1987), 4203.

24. Name Doctor, s.v. "adalia," https://www.name-doctor.com/meaning/adalia.

25. Yodeya, "What Meaning Do the Names . . . ?"

26. Cyrus Alvin Potts, *Dictionary of Bible Proper Names* (New York: Abingdon, 1922), 18.

27. *Old Testament Hebrew Lexicon*, Bible Study Tools, s.v. "Aridatha," accessed December 7, 2023, https://www.biblestudytools.com/lexicons/hebrew/nas/ariydatha.html.

28. *Encyclopedic Dictionary of Bible and Theology*, s.v. "Aridatha," accessed December 7, 2023, https://www.biblia.work/dictionaries/aridatha/.

29. Smith, *Smith's Bible Dictionary*, 483.

30. Yodeya, "What Meaning Do the Names . . . ?"

31. Smith, *Smith's Bible Dictionary*, 53.

32. Yodeya, "What Meaning Do the Names . . . ?"

33. Strong, Hebrew 5172.

34. Brown, Driver, Briggs, 638.

35. NET Bible, s.v. "Ariyday," accessed December 18, 2023, https://classic.net.bible.org/strong.php?id=0742&lang=de.

36. NET Bible, s.v. "Aridai," accessed December 18, 2023, https://classic.net.bible.org/dictionary.php?word=Aridai.

37. Yodeya, "What Meaning Do the Names . . . ?"

38. Smith, *Smith's Bible Dictionary*, 726.

39. *Holman Bible Dictionary*, s.v. "Vajezatha," accessed December 7, 2023, https://www.studylight.org/dictionaries/eng/hbd/v/vajezatha.html.

40. Yodeya, "What Meaning Do the Names . . . ?"

Books by Jane Hamon

Confronting the Thief
Declarations for Breakthrough
Discernment
Dreams and Visions

Jane Hamon serves with her husband, Tom, as senior pastor of Vision Church at Christian International in Santa Rosa Beach, Florida. In their more than 40 years of ministry together, they have built a thriving local church, ministered in more than 65 nations, and helped lead Christian International Ministries, founded by Dr. Bill Hamon.

A clear prophetic voice and eloquent teacher, Jane travels extensively ministering at national and international conferences, consulting with leaders, conducting prophetic workshops, and teaching at Bible colleges. She is featured frequently on a variety of Christian television programs. A gifted storyteller, she sprinkled her five previous books—*Declarations for Breakthrough* (Chosen, 2021), *Discernment* (Chosen, 2019), *Dreams and Visions* (Chosen, 2016), *The Deborah Company* (Destiny Image, 2007), and *The Cyrus Decree* (Christian International, 2001)—with rich personal experiences, extensive research, and biblical teaching.

Jane attended Christ For The Nations Institute in Dallas, Texas, and later received a bachelor of theology and an honorary doctorate of divinity from Christian International School of Theology.

Jane and Tom make their home in beautiful Santa Rosa Beach, Florida, where she enjoys fulfilling some of her favorite roles in life as wife, mother, and now "Mimi" to her growing number of grandchildren.

For further information, please contact Jane at the following:

/ApostleJaneHamon   VisionChurchCI.org

@TomAndJaneHamon   ChristianInternational.com